A Bunch of Fragrant Roses

About the Author

P.P. Ramachandran, 76 years old, is a postgraduate in Economics, postgraduate in Comparative Mythology, and Certificate and Diploma holder in Sanskrit from Mumbai University. He has served in the Reserve Bank of India for 40 years and retired as Deputy General Manager. He writes for a number of journals and is a prolific reviewer of books and a book selector for libraries. He gives lectures regularly to audiences, young and old, on different disciplines. He resides in Mumbai with his wife and two daughters. He is a rare bird—a literary banker. His hobbies are reading, writing, and watching English and Malayalam movies and art-films.

A Bunch of Fragrant Roses

P.P. RAMACHANDRAN

ACADEMIC FOUNDATION
NEW DELHI

www.academicfoundation.com

First published in 2012
by

ACADEMIC FOUNDATION
4772-73 / 23 Bharat Ram Road, (23 Ansari Road),
Darya Ganj, New Delhi - 110 002 (India).
Phones : 23245001 / 02 / 03 / 04.
Fax : +91-11-23245005.
E-mail : books@academicfoundation.com
www.academicfoundation.com

Cataloguing in Publication Data--DK
Courtesy: D.K. Agencies (P) Ltd. <docinfo@dkagencies.com>

Ramachandran, P. P.
A bunch of fragrant roses / P.P. Ramachandran.
p. Cm.
ISBN 9788171889778
ISBN 8171889778

1. Celebrities--India. 2. Celebrities. 3. Books--Reviews. 4. Voyages and travels. 5. Ramachandran, P. P.--Travel. 6. Ramachandran, P. P.--Correspondence. I. Title.

DDC 920.054 23

Typeset by Italics India, New Delhi.
Printed and bound in India.

This book is humbly dedicated to my parents:

my father, SHRI P.V. PARAMESWARAN,
a great teacher, a grand scholar, an impressive singer and
a man of true culture whose impact on me has been phenomenal,
and
my mother SMT. ANANTHALAKSHMY,
a very pious person.

CONTENTS

Book Reviews

Travels

Essays

Correspondence

Foreword

P.P. Ramachandran, 'Chandru' as he is affectionately known, was an official of the Reserve Bank of India for forty years. The stereotyped view of a central banker is that of a dry, humourless person focussed exclusively on his profession. Ramachandran is one of the rare birds, who just cannot be classified into a cubby hole.

Ramachandran's canvas is the whole wide world and he paints life with a vignette and readers will find this collectors' item an unputdownable book. The sheer breadth of his vision is wonderful to the point of bewilderment. In this slim volume, Ramachandran deftly handles subjects as widely variegated as contemporary issues, religion, science, the fine arts, mythology, social issues and biographical sketches.

Ramachandran is a reconnoitre of events and encounters with eminent personalities. He is at his scintillating best handling vastly different subjects, and in one life time he has successively performed as central banker, journalist, social worker, critic, biographer and more.

At the Reserve Bank of India functions he would regale the audience with his amazing memory of events and interaction with prominent personalities. Like the village school master in Oliver Goldsmith's *The Deserted Village*, it could be said of Ramachandran: "And still they gaz'd and still the wonder grew, that one small head could carry all he knew."

Ramachandran's writings are a sonata—a sheaf of memories—and the reader's appetite would be whetted by this book and look forward to future volumes by him. Ramachandran is truly a man for all seasons.

S.S. Tarapore

July 31, 2012

(S.S. Tarapore)

Former Deputy Governor,
Reserve Bank of India;
a columnist and the author of
"Financial Policies in Everyday Life" (AF, 2010).

Preface

This book is the result of the perseverance with which my wife Lakshmy has inspired and prodded me. For five decades I have been writing and publishing articles but never thought of putting a few of them between covers. Her ardent ambition has now been fulfilled.

My drafts were very carefully screened by my elder daughter Priya and son-in-law Gopal. My younger daughter Pushpa and son-in-law Anand patiently transferred my pieces to the computer and ensured that the final product was error free.

I have had the close support of my family and good friends in this effort.

I express my deep gratitude to Shri S.S. Tarapore for writing a scintillating 'Foreword' to my book.

Last but not the least, my thanks flow to Shri Rituraj Kapila, Academic Foundation, who has published my book and has been my friend, guide and philosopher throughout this project.

— P.P. Ramachandran

Preface

People

PEOPLE »

1 Vinda Karandikar

I had the privilege of studying English under Prof Vinda Karandikar in Ramnarain Ruia College over 50 years ago. He taught us Shakespeare's 'Merchant of Venice' and 'Macbeth'. Lo and behold, the characters would spring alive in our classroom, Macbeth brooding in high tension and remorse, and Portia becoming a 'Daniel come to judgement' for the bloodthirsty Shylock.

Prof Karandikar's lectures held us spellbound and he inspired a generation of students. It is quite rarely that we come across instances of eminence being achieved simultaneously in two languages. Karandikar strode like a Colossus through the twin worlds of Marathi poetry and English prose.

Govind Vinayak Karandikar (August 23, 1918—March 14, 2010), better known as Vinda Karandikar, is a well-known Marathi poet and writer. He was the most experimental and comprehensive among all the modern Marathi poets. He was conferred the 39th Jnanpith Award in 2003, which is the highest literary award in India. Conferring the Award in 2006, ex-President A.P.J. Abdul Kalam described him as an essayist, critic and translator, who has made a notable contribution to Marathi poetry and literature. "His life is an example of extraordinary achievement realised through ceaseless search for aesthetic perfection."

Some of the other awards conferred on him included Keshavsut Prize, Soviet Land Nehru Literary Award, Kabir Samman, and the Sahitya Akademi Fellowship in 1996. Karandikar was born on August 23,

1918 at Ghalval village in the present-day Sindhudurg district of Maharashtra. Born to a poor farmer, he went through times of great hardship. He could complete his school and college education from Kolhapur solely due to timely help from a well wisher. He completed his masters degree in English, and went on to settle in Mumbai, choosing teaching as his profession.

Thought provoking subjects like universal truths, mortality, scientific approach and spiritual inclination were the core of his poetry. Vinda did a lot of experimentation in his poems, and he dabbled in different types and compositions of poetry like *ghazals*, songs, *mukta suneet* (free sonnet). His famous collection of poems includes 'Sved Ganga', 'Mruda Gandha', 'Dhrupad', 'Virupika' and 'Jatak'. His collection of short essays, 'Sparshaachi Palav' and 'Akashacha Arth' not only show his unique style of thinking, but also his sharp wit. 'Parampara Ani Navata' is a collection of analytical reviews, which enjoys an important place among the various critiques in Marathi literature.

Vinda wrote many poems for children, different from traditional nursery rhymes. These poems show good understanding of children, their own little world, their imagination, and their ideas. They are especially touching because he has used novel, imaginative, mystical, humorous and unique ideas of children. 'Ranichi Baag', 'Ekda Kaay' 'Jhale', 'Ajabkhana', 'Sarkaswala', and 'Pari Ga Pari' are some of his popular collections that have enriched the world of children.

Two anthologies of his selected poems, 'Sanhita' and 'Adimaya' were also published. He also modernised old Marathi literature like 'Dnyaneshwari' and 'Amrutānubhava'. Besides having been a prominent Marathi poet, Karandikar has contributed to Marathi literature as an essayist, a critic and a translator. Karandikar was the third Marathi writer—after Khandekar and Shirvadkar—to have won the Jnanpith Award for his work called 'Ashtadarshan' (poetry). Vinda, with Vasant Bapat and Mangesh Padgaonkar, travelled all over Maharashtra, organising thousands of poetry reading sessions.

In his book 'Poems of Vinda' there is a very valuable discussion entitled 'Ten Minutes with the Poet', a dialogue between Vinda and Sadanand

Bhatkal. Recalling the earliest incident in his life, the poet, says "I was just a kid. I ran to my mother, to know for certain, whether I had a step mother, whether she had tried to murder the son of a kinsman and whether she was arrested, tried and transported for life—for that was how my playmates teased me. My mother, with tears in her eyes said it was so and added that my step mother was a witch, who deserved hanging. I found myself haunted by a deep sense of sin from which I have never been able to extricate myself."

Vinda's father, who married his mother much later, must have felt socially uprooted. The couple had five daughters and four sons. His father, who had the dignity of a village leader, imbibed the reformist zeal from Savarkar and patriotic fervour from Tilak. Villagers told stories of his fight with a tiger, his risky plunge into a flooded river to save a woman's life, his throwing away his idols into a well in a monotheistic mood, and his courageous facing of a social boycott for his softness to untouchables.

Vinda's translations into English of Shakespeare's 'King Lear', Aristotle's 'Poetics' and the first part of Goethe's 'Faust' are highly praised. Along with A.K. Ramanujan, the eminent poet and folk artist, he translated his own poems into English in two volumes—'Poems of Vinda' and 'More Poems of Vinda'. Adverting to the art of translation of his poems into English, the poet recalls his association with A.K. Ramanujan, who—for Vinda represented a happy combination of poetic genius with linguistic methodology. He gives credit to Ramanujan for his guidance. Later on he got good help from M.V. Rajadhyaksha, R. Parthasarathy and Derek Anto.

Vinda's acceptance speech at the Jnanpith Award function is a classic example of explaining a poet's credo. Here are the cardinal items—"The poet who wants to cope with the variety and complexity of life has no other alternative but to accept an 'open view of poetry'. This accepts the possibility, usefulness and aesthetic significance of different kinds of moods, forms and styles. It does not equate 'purity' with certain states of emotions, or 'beauty' with particular attributes of form. It does not belittle traditional forms and modes in its enthusiasm for experiments, or dub normal moods and attitudes as essentially non-poetic. It admits ugliness, dirt, cruelty and vulgarities, but refuses to worship these as deities...My poetry includes realism and fantasy, a Marxist concern with social reality, and a Freudian concern with sex or the unconscious, satirical outbursts and mystical probings of the ineffable, traditional modes and new experiments. Marxism gives me one more insight into the nature of man and society. It becomes a part of my imaginative awareness of life. I have never conceived myself in the role of an active revolutionary."

Vinda believed in an open view of life, art and literature. "As I was a Professor of English literature, my poetry was influenced by Browning, Hopkins and T.S. Eliot. The three Marathi poets who influenced me were Keshavasut, Madhav Julian and Mardhekar. In my poetry there is a diversity of ideas, which reveals the influence of Marxism and Gandhism, Russell's skepticism and Indian mysticism. For those who believe in self-consistent closed theories, I am a very inconvenient poet."

"I believe in Science, not in Religion. Long ago Bacon said "Knowledge is Power." By knowledge I mean not only knowledge of the world without man but also the knowledge of the world within man and of the society he has brought into being. So Freud or Marx, Lincoln or Gandhi is as much a liberator of man as Darwin or Einstein...Science will create the new man who recognises no distinctions of colour, race, religion, sex or nationality, who stands for the unity and brotherhood of mankind, who believes in freedom, equality and social justice as basic values...He will be an incurable optimist in spite of setbacks."

How munificent was Vinda! He donated over 7 lakh of rupees—the money he earned through prizes—to arrange the Madhav Julian and R.D. Karve Memorial Lectures. During his life, he donated wealth and after death, he donated his body for scientific research.

PEOPLE »

2 Durga Bhagwat

I wish to begin by recounting a charming story of a great son of India, an *asli punekar* Prof D.D. Kosambi. Why do I call him an Asli Punekar? He held the chair for Mathematics at the Tata Institute of Fundamental Research, Bombay from 1946. Yet he would travel every day from his own house at the 'Bori' colony in Poona by Deccan Queen—attend to his lectures, and in the evening board the Deccan Queen—and go back to Poona. This went on for 16 years. Letters used to be delivered to Prof D.D. Kosambi c/o Deccan Queen—including one from Sir John Cockcroft, Chairman of the British A.E.C.—his seat was his only—no one dare occupy it.

Just like Prof Kosambi, letters were delivered to Durgabai c/o Asiatic Library. As a life member of the Asiatic Library from 1956, I myself have seen her for over 40 years ensconced in a green sofa in the foyer of this prestigious library—among the impressive statues of Bartle Frere, John Sargent and Mahamahopadhyaya P.V. Kane. This tiny lady—in a *nauvari sari*—could be seen daily, either writing or lecturing to a small band of admirers, scholars and experts from the various fields of arts. I had guts only to say *namaskar* initially. As I worked in the adjoining Reserve Bank, I used to visit the Asiatic Library daily and have met her quite regularly.

Renowned litteratéur, thinker and staunch proponent of the freedom of expression, Durga Bhagwat was born in Indore in 1910. She passed away in 2002. Besides being a writer and a thinker, she will be remembered in the annals of Marathi literature as a staunch upholder of democracy and for her fiery speech against the emergency that she delivered as the President of the 51st All India Marathi literary meet at Karad. She was jailed, and the country recognised in Bhagwat the 'real' Durga, and in Indira Gandhi the 'artificial' Durga. She campaigned against the ruling Congress party in 1977 general election and remained a staunch enemy till her death. She decided not to accept any state-sponsored honours (with one exception) and declined an offer of Jnanpith Award, the most prestigious award for Indian writers.

Before chairing the Marathi Sahitya Sammelan, she was elected chairperson of the Tamasgir meet—Tamasgirs come typically from young prostitutes. She was proud of this and considered it a great honour.

Bhagwat did her graduation from St Xaviers College, Bombay. She spent six years in the jungles of Madhya Pradesh preparing a thesis on tribals. She is respected for her deep study of our epics 'Ramayana' and 'Mahabharata'. She was conferred the Sahitya Akademi Award in 1972. A tremendous scholar, she was an expert on anthropology, sociology and Buddhist literature. She was proficient in a number of languages—Sanskrit, Pali, Bengali and German, apart from her mastery over Marathi and English.

Her notable works include 'Pais', a collection of articles based around religions, their literature and practices, and 'Vyas Parva', her study of Mahabharata. She was an expert in religious literature, works of Marathi saints from Dyaneshwar to Tukaram, major works of Vyasa Muni and Adi Shankaracharya. Her book 'Rituchakra', describing nature in each Indian month, is her most famous work. Her translation of Siddhartha's 'Jatak Katha' acquired great popularity. Her repertoire also included a cookery book.

She remained a spinster and when asked about it, she told Jaywant Dalvi that she spent several years of her youth in research, during which she was a victim of food poisoning, and that by the time she recovered it was too late. Among her idols were Vyasa Muni,

Adi Shankaracharya, Gautama Buddha, Henry David Thoreau and Shridhar Venkatesh Ketkar.

I have chosen to write about her book 'The Riddle in Indian Life-lore and Literature', which was published in 1965. It is an elaboration of the chapter on the riddle in her Marathi book 'Lokathityachi Ruparekha'— an outline of folklore. It gives concisely the exact picture of the essential forms, features and trends of riddles, both ritualistic and literary, with the relevant cultural background.

Riddles incorporate a question primarily and an answer secondarily. A fact is concealed in the question in the form of a metaphor. The answer reveals the hidden meaning. Concealment is crucial to a riddle. The ultimate purpose of a riddle is to impart knowledge or moral instruction. Riddles have influenced popular imagination more than any other oral tradition. The Indian tradition of riddles is very ancient, even pre-Vedic. It is an ever-alive popular institution, which keeps both people's faith and their wit perennially going on.

Vedic riddles are poetic in form and content, and draw much from the sources of power, mystery, beauty and life itself. This is a sample from the 'Vajaseniya Samhita':

Who wanders lonely on his way?
Who is constantly born anew?
What is the remedy for cold?
What is the great corn vessel called?

Answer:
The sun wanders lonely on its way.
The moon is constantly born anew.
Fire is the remedy for cold.
The earth is the great corn vessel.

Bhagwat goes on to deal with riddles from the 'Mahabharata' onwards. The most famous is the 'Yaksha Prasna', where a critical situation emerges if the right answer is not given. Thus, the four Pandavas are struck dead by the Yaksha. Yudhishtira brings his brothers back to life by answering all questions correctly.

'Prahelika' refers to verses, which conceal the real meaning and suggest another. They are used in conversations of the learned and in witty repartees. A sample:

Paaniyam paathum icchami tvatthah kamalalochane
Di dasyasi nechhamo no dasyasi pibamyaham

Literal meaning:
I wish to drink water from you, O lotus-eyed girl.
If you give me, I do not desire it.
If you do not give, then I drink.

The solution to the riddle is:
I wish to drink water from you, O lotus-eyed girl.
If you are a servant girl, I do not desire it.
If you are not a maid servant, then I shall drink it.

A very popular riddle is 'Samasya'. The first three lines contain one or more questions—the solution comes in the last line. The King would offer the fourth line to the pundits and they were asked to supply the first three lines. The most famous and tragic Samasya led to the death of Kalidasa.

Once the King of Ceylon, Kumarasena, a friend of Kalidasa, declared a riddle and offered to give a handsome reward to one who solved it. The riddle was:

Kusume kusumothpatthi sruyathe na cha drisyathe

"That a flower is born of a flower, is heard of, but not seen"

Kalidasa, who was in Ceylon, heard the riddle from a courtesan and composed the solution in one line:

Bale tava mukhamboje katham indivaradvayam

"O Girl, how is it that on the lotus of your face there are two blue lotuses (of the eyes)?"

The courtesan killed the poet and went to the king and demanded the prize. The King detected the Kalidasa touch, found out how the riddle had caused his friend's death and jumped into the funeral pyre of the poet and was burnt to death. King Bhoja was another such king famous for his Samasyas.

Durga Bhagwat has an interesting chapter on the riddle and the proverb. In Sanskrit as well as other languages, there are a large number of poems describing various Gods. Apparently these are about finite Gods from the Epics and Puranas, but actually these refer to the man who has received the 'master key' (*guru-killi*).

The meaning would be entirely different. She gives an example of a Marathi verse of Jnanadeva (13th century),

"God Vitthala quarrelled with his consort Rakhumai, and who will put a stop to their quarrel now? It is Jnanadeva, humble at the feet of Nivritti (elder brother and teacher of Jnanadeva), who will do it."

The meaning of such verses is not so simple. Names as Vithala, Rakhumai are to be interpreted as Brahma and Maya, and the names of Nivritti and Jnanadeva are to be treated as common nouns meaning renunciation and knowledge, respectively. The verse will mean now—the eternal soul—Brahman or self—*atman* is always in conflict with *maya*—illusion which causes all delusion and makes things appear differently from what it actually is.

Who will stop this conflict?

It is knowledge alone with renunciation.

PEOPLE »

3 T.N. Shanbag

We have assembled in such large numbers to mourn the sad demise of Shri T.N. Shanbag, founder of Strand Book Stall and to pray that his soul rests in peace.

In a celebrated phrase at a spectacular send-off, held in Westminster, to the lion that roared—Sir Winston Churchill, Prime Minister, Clement Attlee (the mouse that squeaked) declared, "I come to praise Caesar, not to bury him."—happily reversing Mark Antony. I shall echo the words of Attlee and praise Shri Shanbag, who passed away on February 27, 2009.

To begin at the beginning. The year is 1956. The month—December. The date—4th. It is a memorable day for me for two reasons. That was my first day in the Reserve Bank of India (RBI)—where I served for 40 long years. Second reason is that was the day when I met Shanbag for the first time—and the association continued for over 52 years and a quarter. I wonder if anyone in this August assembly has a longer link with Shanbag. If yes, my *pranams* to him or her! When I bought my first book from Shanbag, his son Arun was five months young and his daughter Vidya had not yet arrived!

Strand Book Stall was then only half as spacious as it is today—no mezzanine floor. Shanbag welcomed me with his customary cherubic smile. He did not have more than 500 books then. He had arranged—flat facing you—copies of *Encounter* magazine. "Young man", he said, "you should read 'Encounter'. It is a monthly edited by the British poet laureate Stephen Spender and the political analyst Irving Kristol." I became an addict. I drank deeply the articles of Arthur Koestler on Galileo Galilei and Tycho Brahe in his 'Sleepwalkers' and also the thrilling series of Bertrand Russell— 'My Philosophical Development'. Shanbag led me on from *Encounter* to *New Statesman and Nation* edited then by Kingsley Martin. From periodicals to books was, but, a short jump with a strong push from Shanbag.

He asked me as to where I worked and when I told him "This is my first day in RBI", he beamed and recounted his association with book lovers from RBI. He told me of how he lugged eight volumes of Will and Ariel Durant's 'Story of Civilisation' and sold 50 sets to staff of RBI. Its price—a mere Rs 500. Since RBI staff got only a monthly pay of Rs 158, he allowed them 10 monthly instalments of Rs 50. Years later I bought the complete set from him—three more volumes added by the historic couple—at a whopping Rs 10,000.

I learnt from him that he began his voyage with a capital of Rs 450 in November 1948. During the interval of the Clifton Webb starrer film Cheaper by the Dozen in the Strand theatre in Colaba, Shanbag saw an attractive corner in the foyer of that theatre. Promptly after the show was over Shanbag went to see Keki Modi, owner of Strand and 55 other theatres, and revealed to him his plan to start a book stall and requesting for a little space in his theatre. Modi was amused but bowled over by the youth's enthusiasm, gave him the space with a smile, thus encouraging him. That small beginning has led to today's most reputed stall in India with a branch in Bangalore run by his daughter and a recently opened outlet at Infosys, Pune—exclusively for them.

When Shanbag wanted to acquire the present place at Dhannur, the owner Shri V.H. Gumaste, the Chief Public Prosecutor, insisted on a good reference—preferably from the Bombay High Court. Shanbag got one from the Chief Justice Shri M.C. Chagla who wrote, "Shri Shanbag is not only a clean young man but he is my bookseller." Rest is history.

The first book Shanbag sold was Winston Churchill's 'War Memoirs'—the first copy of which he sold to Richard Burton, Chief Executive of

Stanvac on 20th November, 1948 and at a discount of 20 per cent. The discounts have continued for 60 years. Beginning with Churchill—slowly but steadily—Shanbag made magnificent strides in selection of titles. Shanbag was the only bookseller to offer a minimum discount of 20 per cent on all titles—more on select titles. He declared that—"a book seller acts as a catalyst between a book and the reading habit." He realised that discounted prices increased the sales and brought more profits. He spoke of being devoted more to Goddess Saraswati and less to Goddess Lakshmi.

Always immaculately attired in a full suit with a matching tie, Shanbag had a Pickwickian personality with a slight paunch, a shining dome and perennial smile. He was a true friend, guide and philosopher. He had a way with customers that those who came 'just to have a look' went home with a book. He had an encyclopedic knowledge and could recommend books on a number of disciplines.

As the cornucopia of books was ushered in, so also the number of distinguished regular buyers of eminence grew. All of us are aware of the nocturnal visit of Jawaharlal Nehru. M.O. Mathai rang up Shanbag and told him that the Prime Minister (PM) wishes to come to his Stall. What would be the best hour? Replied Shanbag,"Let him come at 10.30 pm. No red lights and sirens blaring, as we are in a residential area." Nehru arrived at 10.30, spent an hour and picked up 23 books. To show his gratitude, Shanbag invited Keki Modi to be present when Nehru landed in Strand Book Stall. Modi was overjoyed to spend some memorable time with Nehru.

Shanbag was introduced to Sarvepalli Radhakrishnan, by his grandson Shri M. Narasimham, later Governor of RBI. Dr Radhakrishnan introduced Shanbag to his publisher Stanley Unwin. In turn, he led him on to Sir Allen Lane, the publisher of 'Penguin' and 'Pelican' books. He got into the world of Bertrand Russell and other great British intellectuals.

Strand Book Stall achieved an iconic status and we had a stream of great men and women visiting it. I had the privilege of meeting a number of them and obtaining autographs in their books. To name a few, Satyajit Ray, Vikram Seth, Dominique Lapierre, Pico Iyer, Mahaswetha Devi, Shyam Benegal, etc. The Three Musketeers of the *Times of India*—Shamlal, Inder Malhotra and R.K. Laxman would come every Friday at lunch time and discuss about various books with Shanbag.

I must not fail to mention two books published by Strand, which had phenomenal sales. One was 'We, the Nation' by Nani Palkhivala and the other was 'The New Landscape' by Charles Correa. This added a feather to Shanbag's cap.

Shanbag arranged extremely successful book exhibitions at Sunderbai Hall and also in Bangalore. Thousands of book lovers would sweep down and grab tonnes of books at special discounted rates.

In 2003, the Government of India conferred on Shanbag the Padma Shri, which I felt was a perfect example of 'too little and too late'.

Shanbag has ensured that his spirit will be kept burning fiercely by a band of dedicated staff. My good friend Shenvi—the current manager and his able lieutenants will instantly give you books on the premises. Those not readily available will be made available by a vigorous search. A visit to Strand is like a visit to a religious place of pilgrimage. One gets solace, peace and wisdom—with discounts too!

Abraham Lincoln once wrote to a mother whose sons had perished in the war, "I feel how weak and fruitless must be any words of mine which should attempt to beguile you from the grief of a loss so overwhelming." This is equally true here. The loss the Shanbag family has sustained is shared by a large circle of friends and admirers of Shanbag.

I mourn the loss of a very good friend—the true disciple of Goddess Saraswati. I have no doubt that Shanbag must be now sitting in the lap of Goddess Saraswati and blessing all of us with his beatific smile.

PEOPLE »

4 Albert Einstein

Albert Einstein is one of the greatest icons of our age: The kindly refugee from oppression whose wild halo of hair, twinkling eyes, engaging humanity and extraordinary brilliance made his face a symbol and his name a synonym for genius.

Albert Einstein was born at Ulm in Germany in 1879. His father was an electrical engineer, who one day brought a compass for his young son. Einstein trembled with excitement as he saw the 'magic needle' turning towards the north! The fact that the magnetic needle behaved as if influenced by some hidden force field produced a sense of wonder that motivated him throughout his life. Einstein would retain for ever the intuition and awe of a child. He never lost his sense of wonder at the magic of nature's phenomena—magnetic fields, gravity, inertia, acceleration, light beams—which grown-ups find commonplace. "People like you and me never grow old", he wrote to a friend. "We never cease to stand like curious children before the great mystery into which we were born."

His mother, an accomplished pianist, also gave him a gift at around the same time—a violin—one that would last throughout his life. She arranged for him to take violin lessons. Music moved him. As his mother played a Mozart or Beethoven sonata, he would stand in a trance. Einstein told his son that whenever he felt that he had come to the end of the road or faced a difficult challenge in his work, he would take refuge in music and that would solve all his difficulties.

His teachers told his father that the boy was mentally slow, adrift in his foolish dreams. They called him 'Pater Langweil'—Father Bore. He was a lonely child except for the company of books. He had mastered the works of Euclid, Newton, Spinoza and Descartes before he was 15. He decided to specialise in Mathematics. He finished his studies and got his teacher's certificate, but had no job as he was a Jew. One day his teacher brought a large nail to the class and said, "The nails with which Jesus was nailed to the cross looked like this." As the only Jew in class of 70 students, one can imagine the impact of such a demonstration by his teacher.

Since he had some difficulty in getting a University job, he joined the Swiss Patent Office in Bern. In the mornings, Einstein worked on patents but in the afternoons, secreting his books under his desk, he began to formulate the theories that would revolutionise science. He published five papers in 1905, while he was still unknown at the Patent Office. His most striking contribution to Science came not from work in the laboratory, but from what he called 'thought experiments'. The Special Theory of Relativity came from one such brilliant idea. The General Theory of Relativity, considered Einstein's greatest achievement came from another thought experiment—he called it the happiest thought of his life. The General Theory completely changed the way we look at the universe. Two British expeditions proved in 1919 that Einstein's prediction of the deflection of light was accurate. Einstein found himself famous and the fame never abated. He got the Nobel Prize in 1921, not for his theories on relativity but 'for his services to theoretical physics, and especially for his discovery of the law of the photoelectric effect'.

In 1903 he married Mileva Maric, a fellow student at the University of Zurich. She did not complete her studies as she had become pregnant with Einstein's child while they were still students. She gave birth to an illegitimate daughter. Einstein and Mileva had two sons after they were married. The marriage fell apart as Einstein fell in love with his cousin. He divorced Mileva and in that settlement, Einstein promised her his share of the Nobel Prize, three years before he was to win it. Note his self-confidence of winning the Nobel! We have a similar example of C.V. Raman who booked two tickets by boat to Stockholm—for himself and his wife—even before the prize for the year 1930 was announced. Great is the confidence of great men!

In the early 1930s, Einstein left Germany for America. He later urged the United States to develop the atom bomb before Germany did the same. Although he had no connection with the building of the bombs, which were to destroy Hiroshima and Nagasaki, after Hiroshima he said, "If I had known they were going to do this, I would have become a shoe maker."

Though he became world famous, he continued to be a simple man. Once the Queen of Belgium invited him to pay her a visit. Never suspecting that a reception committee would be waiting for him at the railway station, Einstein alighted from the train with a suitcase in one hand and a violin in the other, and set on foot to the Queen's palace. "Why did you not come in the car I sent to you, Herr Doktor?" asked the Queen. Answered Einstein, "It was a pleasant walk, Your Majesty."

Once a young student asked him to explain Relativity Theory in simple language. Einstein said, "When you are in your maths class one hour looks like one year but if you are playing football one hour appears to be one minute. That is relativity." On another occasion, the Professor was in his house in Princeton. It was Christmas time. A batch of carol singers knocked at his door. He asked what they were doing. They said they were singing carols and collecting money for the poor. "Wait a minute" said the Nobel Prize winner and came back with his violin and said, "I am joining you."

Occasionally, Einstein would take rambling walks on his own in Princeton. One day someone called the Institute and asked to speak to a particular Dean. When his Secretary said that the Dean wasn't available, the caller asked for Einstein's home address. That was not possible to give, he was informed. The caller's voice then dropped to a whisper. "Please don't tell anybody", he said, "but I am Dr Einstein, I'm on my way home, and I have forgotten where my house is". He was a truly simple man.

He died in 1955 of heart failure, shortly after calling for his pen and latest page of calculations. The *New York Times* wrote an obituary note and said, "Man stands on this diminutive earth, gazes at the myriad stars and upon billowing oceans and tossing trees—and wonders. What does it all mean? How did it all come about? The most thoughtful wanderer who appeared among us in three centuries has passed on in the person of Albert Einstein."

5 Two Giants of Science: Michael Faraday and Marie Curie

Michael Faraday

Michael Faraday stumbled into science from the humblest and most unlikely beginning. A bookbinder's apprentice, he became a man who commanded the intellectual society of England.

In 1857, Michael Faraday (1791-1867) had arrived at what most men would regard as a summit of achievement. He was offered the Presidency of the Royal Society. But the most brilliant scholar of his generation refused the honour. He said, "I must remain plain Mr Faraday to the last." He is famous for his experiments in electromagnetism, the conversion of electricity into power, and into light. Many consider him the greatest experimentalist who ever lived. Several concepts that he derived from experiments, such as lines of magnetic force, have become common ideas of today's modern physics. He sent his notes of a lecture made by Humphrey Davy to the Scientist. As a result of this he was appointed, at the age of 21, assistant to Davy in the laboratory of the Royal Institution in London. His father was a blacksmith, uncle a grocer, and one brother a plumber. When Gladstone met Michael Faraday, he asked him whether his work on electricity would be of any use, "Yes, Sir", remarked Faraday with prescience, "One day you will tax it."

One day an employee of the Royal Mint, a certain Joseph Newton, was sent down to perform an experiment at the laboratory of the Royal

Institution. He noticed an old man, dressed in a shabby suit, observing him with a whimsical smile.

"I suppose", said Newton, "you have been here for a number of years?"

"Yes. A good many years."

Newton - "Sort of janitor?"

"Yes, sort of."

"I hope they pay you well?"

"I could stand a little better pay."

"And, what, my man, is your name?"

"Michael Faraday."

Plain Michael Faraday to the last.

Marie Curie

Marie Curie, arrived in Paris with little but determination and brilliance, which was to net her two Nobel Prizes and a place, literally in the 'Pantheon'.

Madame Curie (1867-1934) was a Pole. Her father a Professor of physics, and mother a pianist. She married Pierre Curie, a French scientist. They were both recipients of Nobel Prizes. The Curies were simple people and made efforts to escape fame. They did not attend the ceremony where the Nobel Prize was awarded, but were working in their laboratory.

Marie's simple disguise for avoiding recognition was to remain undisguised. Nobody at first sight would have suspected that the young peasant woman in her unassuming black dress was a Nobel laureate. One day an American reporter, hot on the trail of the Curies had heard that they were spending their vacation in 'Le Pouldu', found the way to their cottage and saw a plain woman sitting barefoot on the doorsteps.

"Are you the housekeeper?"

"Yes."

"Is the lady inside?"

"No. She is out."

"Do you expect her soon?"

"I don't think so."

"Could you tell something intimate about her?"

"Nothing", replied Marie, "except one message that Madam asked me to convey to reporters - that is

"Be less inquisitive about people and more inquisitive about ideas."

One rainy morning in April 1906, Pierre Curie left his home to meet his publisher. A few hours later they brought his lifeless body to Marie. He had slipped on the wet road and a heavy truck had run over him.

She accepted her husband's place in the University of Sorbonne—it was the first time in French history that a position in higher education had been granted to a woman. In 1911, she received the Nobel Prize for the second time. She died of radium poisoning—the gradual decay of the vital organs through a lifetime of excessive radiation. She died a martyr to science.

I shall conclude with the famous quatrain of H.W. Longfellow.

"Lives of great men all remind us
We can make our lives sublime,
And, departing leave behind us
Foot prints on the sands of time"

PEOPLE »

6 Majestic and Serene: M.S.

M.S. represents the highest achievement in Carnatic music by one who transmuted melody into *bhakti*.

Madurai, the temple town, connected with Agastya Muni, the seat and fount of *sangams* was the place from where were born the mother —M. Shanmukhavadivu and the daughter M.S. Subbulakshmi. The 'M' in the initials of both the names was more than a geographical formality. It was an umbilical chord that bound them with culture. Subbulakshmi attracted attention transcending music itself. She grew into a unique phenomenon in Tamil culture, combining the vitality of *dravida* heritage with the rich resonance of sanskritic traditions. M.S. honored the ancientness of tradition, anchored her art on a spiritual basis and absorbed the best in others while developing her own distinctiveness.

M.S. was one of the three children of Shanmukhavadivu, the other two being an elder brother M.S. Shaktivel and a younger sister M.S. Vadivambal. M.S. only had a pet name—Kunjamma or Kunju. Shaktivel became adept in playing *mridangam*. Vadivambal took after her mother and became a *veena* player of promise. M.S., however, excelled in *veena* and *mridangam* and got the special attention of her mother. The first *guru* to teach M.S. was Madurai Srinivasa Iyengar. Two others succeeded him—Seithur Sundaresa Bhattar and Mayavaram Krishna Iyer. Subbulakshmi was a little over nine when her mother asked her to sing at a gathering organised by a cycle shop, which eventually became the huge TVS (T.V. Sundaram) conglomerate.

A talent-spotter in the audience approached the family with an offer of cutting a gramophone record, which was promptly accepted. The song HMV recorded under its twin brand was 'Marakata Vadivu' in *Chenchuruti raga*, praising Madurai Meenakshi. The label on the record read: "Song by Madurai Subbulakshmi, age 10 years." The singer says at the end of the song, "I am Madurai Subbulakshmi."

Shanmukhavadivu used to take her two daughters for programmes in the courts of the wealthy and influential. One of them sought the hand of Vadivambal—a millionaire Bhashyam Iyengar. Soon after the marriage, Vadivambal died of pneumonia at the young age of 22. Meanwhile, M.S. had moved over to Madras. A quick succession of events catapulted her to eminence. She won recognition in citadels of music and started making it big in the movies.

M.S. achieved laurels at 16 at the Kumbakonam Mahamaham in 1932. Here she was lauded by veterans like Tiger Varadachari, Muthiah Bhagavathar and Chembai Vaidyanatha Bhagavathar. Karaikudi Sambasiva Iyer told M.S., "Child, you carry the Veena in your throat". She followed this up by storming the male bastion—The Madras Music Academy during 1932-33. At the young age of 17, M.S. had become a musical star.

Enter Thiagaraja Sadasivam. In the year 1936 when she was 20, Sadasivam who was 34—senior to her by 14 years—entered her life. He was already married and had two children, whom M.S. brought up as her own. Sadasivam and M.S. got married in 1940 and lived happily for 57 years till Sadasivam passed away at his 95th year. Author T.J.S. George in his book titled 'M.S.: life in music' has eloquently summed up the connection between the duo.

"Never did a couple fill each other's life as completely as Sadasivam and M.S. did. Never did another husband visualise, orchestrate and control his wife's career as decisively as Sadasivam did. Never did a man transform a woman's life as totally as Sadasivam transformed M.S.'s. Without Sadasivam, M.S. might just have been a face in the crowd, a great voice among several voices. With him she became

'Queen of Music', a title bestowed by Jawaharlal Nehru. If M.S. made melody, Sadasivam made M.S.. If music was M.S.'s career, M.S. became Sadasivam's career. Never did a husband and wife owe more to each other than Sadasivam and M.S. did."

Her husband carefully introduced her to the tinsel world with K. Subramanyam's Seva Sadanam. This and the next venture Shakuntalai found M.S. an essentially classical singer. It was after the completion of Shakuntalai that M.S. would get married to Sadasivam. She acted in only two more films—Savithri and Meera (in Tamil and Hindi). Sadasivam rung down the curtain on M.S. as an actor after Meera. She devoted the rest of her life to becoming a singer-saint as laid down by Sadasivam.

Some of the songs sung by M.S. in Savithri proved to be all-time hits. The greatest was 'Broohi Mukundeti' of Sadasiva Brahmendra in *Kurunji raga*. Sadasivam used to recount how artists and technicians in New Theatres at Calcutta flocked to hear M.S. whenever there was a recording, and they included K.L. Saigal, Kanan Bala, Pahari Sanyal and Pankaj Mullick. They would request her to sing their favourite songs. About Meera it was rightly said, "M.S. did not act. She became Meera herself in the film." Sarojini Naidu, appearing at the end of the Hindi version declared, "She is not an interpreter but Meera herself."

Sadasivam had a close circle of great friends—Kalki Krishnamurthy, C. Rajagopalachari and Semmangudi Srinivasa Iyer. Rajaji had approved of and blessed Sadasivam's marriage to M.S. The couple came under the spell and protection of the Paramacharya of Kanchi, who accepted the couple as his lifetime *bhaktas*. He gave the highest tribute to M.S.—"Whatever she is, she is like Brindavan Tulasi". The Sadasivams, in turn, venerated him as God. This equation underscored society's acceptance of M.S.'s transformation into an Iyer wife.

The remarkable attribute of M.S. is that her repertoire included compositions of Tulsidas, Surdas, Kabir and Guru Nanak. She spent a lot of time in learning *thumris* and *khayals* from stalwarts like Siddheshwari Devi of Benaras and Dwijendarlal Roy of Calcutta. *Bhakti* became the hallmark of M.S. The art of singing, which she perfected acquired a new direction. She would get soaked in *bhakti* which welled up in her heart every time she sang a composition or *sloka* expressing intense *bhakti* for God. Her rendering of Suprabathams, Vishnu Sahasranamam, Bhaja Govindam and Hanuman Chalisa are actually representative of her oeuvre. M.S. single-handedly transformed the culture of morning prayers across South India.

Sadasivam made M.S. a world phenomenon—arranging concerts at Edinburgh, Paris and Moscow, and culminating in the ultimate recital at United Nations. In the last venue she sang a Rajaji composition—'Kurai Ondrum Illai'—I have no regrets. Mahatma Gandhi was so much fascinated by her voice that once he conveyed a request that she should sing for him the Meera *bhajan* 'Hari Tum Haro'. Unfortunately, she had not learnt this song and conveyed her regrets. Later, the same evening another message came from Gandhiji that he would prefer to hear the song sung by M.S. than by anyone else. Sadasivam arranged immediately for a composer and overnight she learnt the song, recorded it and sent the same to Bapuji. It was played for him on his birthday on 2nd October, 1947. A few months later, the radio announced the shocking news of Gandhiji's assassination. This was followed by the rendering by M.S. of the Meera *bhajan*. M.S swooned on hearing it and for over a year she would not attempt to sing 'Hari Tum Haro'.

M.S. lived a full life with awards heaped on her from all over the globe. All these she placed at the feet of her Lord and mentor Sadasivam. To everyone's lasting regret, the Bharat Ratna was awarded to her a little after Sadasivam's passing away. It was an appropriate reward for his lifetime struggle to keep M.S. always at a pinnacle. Radhakrishnan declared, "Her music is a gift of the Gods which she placed at the service of the Nation."

One of the most poignant scenes in the book 'M.S.' by George is the passing away of Sadasivam, which will bring tears to the eyes of the readers. It is worth recalling in full. "On 19th November 1997 Sadasivam felt something he had never felt before—fluctuating fever and some breathlessness. Reluctantly, he agreed to go to a nursing home for a check-up. He would be back home in three days, he assured his family. The hospital diagnosed his condition to be pneumonia. On the morning of 21st November, he asked for the three rows of *vibhuti* to be applied on his forehead with customary punctiliousness. Coffee arrived from home as per his specifications—dark, hot and sweet, but sipping the brew was not easy, what with the tubes emerging from an oxygen cylinder claiming closer attachment. As the hours of discomfort passed desultorily, an aide noticed his eyes turning glassy. M.S. was sent for. As she entered the room, Sadasivam looked at her, smiled and held her hand. Looking, smiling and holding hands, his eyes glazed over and the breathing stopped. It was so quiet a passing that it took a few moments for those around him to realise that Sadasivam was no more."

One word that frequently cropped up in the language of those who met M.S. in her later years was 'glow'. Everyone talked about how she glowed from within. She was one who had found 'serenity'. An aura of 'grace' surrounded her.

7 S. Chandrasekhar

'Chandra', as Subrahmanyan Chandrasekhar was called, was born in Lahore in 1910. He enrolled himself at 19, with a scholarship, as a graduate student at Trinity College, Cambridge. Nephew of the Nobel Prize winner C.V. Raman, Chandra received a fine education at Presidency College, Madras, and graduated with acclaim—publishing papers in leading journals and impressing eminent visiting scientists from Europe. Chandra could properly have aspired to a spectacular career—physics was in an exhilarating and revolutionary phase in the early 1930s, and Cambridge was the Mecca of scientists.

Before touching Cambridge, Chandra had mastered the seminal work of Arthur Eddington, "The Internal Constitution of the Stars". Eddington was a kind of father figure in theoretical astronomy and when Chandra enrolled at Trinity, he was a Fellow. The two established seemingly cordial relations. Chandra's exceptional talent was plain to all. Chandra had his 'big idea'—that, if Einstein was correct, stars would end their lives in such bizarre, mysterious ways, but this idea remained dormant for three years.

Chandra summoned the courage to present his radical thoughts at the January 1935 meeting of the Royal Astronomical Society. These monthly occasions were the prime arena for discussing new astronomical discoveries. Chandra gave a 30-minute lecture on white dwarf stars. His talk included the suggestion that stars of a certain mass, when they burned out, might collapse forever—their gravitation is so great that not even light could escape it. When Chandra finished his talk, Eddington rose and demolished the notion. "I think there should be a law of Nature to prevent a star from behaving in this absurd way!"

Sir Arthur Eddington, the founder of modern astrophysics, and the man best situated to grasp Chandra's theory, declared that if physics could posit such an incredible notion, then physics was wrong. His counter arguments may have seemed thin, but his authority carried weight with many there.

For the next nine years, Eddington poured ridicule on Chandra and his concepts. Half a century had to elapse before Chandra won the Nobel his work deserved. However, the two men remained professionally cordial. Chandra wrote to his older colleague regularly, and Eddington supported the Indian astrophysicist's nomination to the Royal Society in 1944.

Chandra was intellectually active till he turned 84, but his scientific genius bloomed on his first journey by ship to England. While his ship steamed through the Arabian Sea, he pondered an arcane problem: What happens to stars when they use up all their nuclear fuel? It was thought that a 'dead' star turned into a so-called 'white dwarf'—a dense cinder that could no longer shine. Chandra mastered the theory underlying these concepts, and discovered an enigma. White dwarf stars much heavier than the sun couldn't exist. So what happened to them? According to Einstein's relativity, their gravity would pull them ever inwards, making a 'hole' in space. This fate should have overtaken millions of stars in our galaxy—space should be 'punctured' by huge numbers of black holes.

An American writer, Miller notes the ironies of the background of the two adversaries—the 'humble Indian' scientist came from a family of highly educated men and women of science and letters (his mother translated Ibsen into Tamil; an uncle won the Nobel Prize in 1930), while the haughty Cambridge don was born a Quaker and raised by a single mother following his father's death when the boy was only two.

Chandra left England in 1936 for the University of Chicago, which remained his base until his death at 84. He worked incessantly; he was famous for his stamina in immensely detailed algebraic calculations. He also produced a series of impressive treatises. For decades he avoided the subject that had led him into such traumatic controversy. But when he was in his sixties, he deployed his formidable talents again on the study of black holes. The resultant book, 'The Mathematical Theory of Black Holes', published when he was 72, was the one he found most taxing and challenging to write. It is by any standards a monumental achievement: 650 pages of dense mathematics.

The greatness of Chandra lay in the fact that he bore no grudge against Eddington, who had blocked his Nobel by 50 years. When Eddington died in 1944, Chandra delivered a memorial speech at the University of Chicago. In it he said: "I believe that anyone who has known Eddington will agree that he was a man of the highest integrity and character." In 1982, Cambridge University invited Chandra to deliver a series of lectures on the occasion of Eddington's centenary. He titled it: 'Eddington: The Most Distinguished Astrophysicist of His Time'. For Chandra, his disappointment of the past was over a long, long time ago.

A final charming story about Chandrashekar's commitment to science. Twice a week during the terms of 1948 and 1949, Chandrasekhar made the arduous three hour drive from Yerkes to the Chicago campus to teach a course on astrophysics to just two students, Tsung-dao Lee and Chen Ning Yang. The course was the only physics class in history in which every student won the Nobel Prize. Lee and Yang won the Nobel Prize in 1957. Their Professor, Chandra, waited another 26 years to get his Nobel in 1983.

PEOPLE »

8 Dwaram Venkataswamy Naidu

Dwaram Venkataswamy Naidu, affectionately called Dwaramgaru was born on Diwali in Bangalore on November 3, 1893 and was raised in Visakhapatnam. He was appointed Professor of violin in the Maharaja's Music College in Vizianagaram, at the young age of 26, and became its Principal in 1936. He was the first one to start violin solo concerts. His first solo concert was held in Vellore in 1938. Unfortunately, he was partially blind. He cautioned his disciples against missing practice even for a day. "If you don't practice for one day, you will notice your mistakes, if you don't practice for two days the audience would notice your mistakes!"

Dwaram was a quiet genius. His music sparkles of sublime beauty and grace. His music is a stream of fresh melody in a world obsessed with rhythmic emphasis. S.V. Krishnamurthy of the 'Hindu'—a famous music critic remarks, "The hallmark of Dwaram Venkataswami Naidu's violin is that he soared to the very pinnacle of melodic excellence with the minimum use of technical paraphernalia. His style was stately, reposeful and abounded in tonal mellifluence." Dwaram sculpts the *raga* with a beautiful form in mind. He attempts to create an elegant *raga*, without indulging in 'body-building exercises' in the scale. His goal is an innately handsome *raga*, and not a muscleman. A Dwaram piece stays in your active memory for a long time. He has this innate knack of letting his music ruminate in the minds of his listeners. That is a rare virtue. At a higher level, he was a true *nadopasaka*. Dwaram's music is a sensitive reminder that truly great music utilises the technical apparatus to achieve a greater goal—to take the listener to a plane of sheer aesthetic bliss. Dwaram does just that and effortlessly, like a mother's lullaby to her irate child. Dwaramgaru was one of the greatest violin players of the country. His contemporaries were Rajamanikkam Pillai, Papa Venkataramiah and T. Chowdiah. He was the most famous violinist of Andhra. The family had *bhajan* sessions and though he had a good voice, he was attracted by his elder brother's violin on which he played secretly. His brother did not reprimand him, but gave him lessons in earnest. He began his schooling in Vishakapatnam, and his extreme near-sightedness almost to the level of blindness troubled him and an un-understanding and unsympathetic teacher made his life miserable. His grandfather withdrew him from school and he was tutored at home. This school, the Anglo Vernacular School became the Mrs A.V.N. College and subsequently, the Hindu College, which proudly proclaims Dwaram as its alumnus. At a concert years later, the teacher who had insulted him was moved by his performance and came up to him begging for his pardon.

Dwaram gave mini recitals in the neighbourhood. In 1919, Dwaram enrolled in the Maharaja's College, Vizianagaram, the only college that offered a degree in Music in entire Madras Presidency. The Maharaja and the Principal of the college were so much impressed by Dwaram's performance that they offered him the post of a Professor.

A firm believer in physical fitness, he devised his own exercises. He would teach at the college from 8 am to 10 am and return home to practise on the violin. Every evening he gave performances at home. His listeners included Sarojini Naidu, Harindranath Chattopadhyaya and Dr S. Radhakrishnan. So impressed on hearing him was Rabindranath Tagore that he sang Rabindra *sangeet* to Dwaram's violin accompaniment.

He was master of songs in Tamil, Sanskrit, Telugu and rendered Thiruppugazh and Thevarams. Mali on flute would practice to Dwaram's accompaniment on the *kanjira* or violin. Later Dwaram's daughter

Mangathayaru became a regular accompanist for Mali. Honours were showered on Dwaram. He was conferred the Sangitha Kalanidhi by the Madras Music Academy. The courts of Mysore and Travancore made him *aasthana vidwan*. In 1948, a *sammana mahotsavam* was arranged for him in Madras by Raju, a legislator. A purse of Rs 35,000 was collected and presented to him. Dwaram laid down two conditions for accepting this award. First, he wanted Rs 2,000 to be given to his elder brother and *guru* Venkatakrishnayya. Another Rs 2,000 was to be given to the violinist who had written damagingly about him in the 1920s. With the balance amount he bought a house near Parthasarathy temple, Triplicane. His daughter continues to live there today. He was awarded the Kala Prapurna, and also a Doctorate by the Andhra government. He also received the Sangeet Natak Akademi Award and the Padma Shri. Statues of this great musician have been erected in Visakhapatnam and Chennai. Government of India has issued a postal stamp in his honour on his birth centenary year—1993. I shall conclude with a poignant story about two great violinists. During the 1954 visit of Yehudi Menuhin, Dwaram attended his performance with Justice Rajamannar. After the programme, the judge took Dwaram backstage and introduced him to Menuhin. Dwaram with his fascination for European violins wanted to touch Menuhin's instrument. But the latter would not agree. Rajamannar was upset and arranged a concert the very next evening by Dwaram and invited Menuhin. At the end of the performance, Menuhin was so amazed at Dwaram's mastery that he walked up to him, took him by the hand and apologised for the brusqueness of the previous day. Dwaram was not only allowed to touch Menuhin's violin, but also play to his heart's content.

He was awarded the Andhra Pradesh Sangeeth Natak Akademi Award on the 20th November, 1964 and played the violin after accepting the award. That same night he died of a heart attack.

One last item. Ending on a happy note. Dwaram was so fond of his grandchildren that he would stun them with difficult feats on the violin and get them dancing to folk tunes. When they laughed he would reproduce their laughter on the violin. He would suspend his violin from his collar behind his back and keeping the bow behind, would play that way.

Book Reviews

9 Courting Destiny

When we read fairy tales as young kids we were impressed by Jack, the Giant Killer and David and Goliath from the Bible. In Indian legal history, a similar aura attachés to Shanti Bhushan who brought down her imperial highness Smt Indira Gandhi from her exalted position of the Prime Minister (PM) of India. The book under review is the extraordinary account of the life and times of one of the most illustrious legal luminaries of our nation. It is an account of his family history, experience of a joint family in Uttar Pradesh (UP), his introduction to the world of law, and his distinguished legal career culminating in his becoming a Minister for Law in the Union Cabinet.

The account of his growing years is laced with exquisite stories of great human warmth and how he distinguished himself in the legal world. We have vignettes of Allahabad from which sprang some of the best lawyers and judges in our country. Shanti Bhushan has over six decades of experience in the legal world during which he never was overawed by anyone, however tall. In fact, he had the guts to admonish the Presiding Judge Justice Dwivedi, who had erred in passing an order in one case. He said, "I had half a mind to move a formal application for contempt proceedings against your Lordship for making that order." He was the one, totally committed to his convictions and never bent to please anyone.

Shanti Bhushan; Penguin/Viking; pp. 395; Price Rs 650/-

Shanti Bhushan gives an interesting and gripping account of the Keshav Singh case of 1964, which led to the first stand-off between the executive and the judiciary. He provides a succinct account of the political events from the late 1960s to the decline and fall of the Janata Party government. Of extraordinary interest is his brilliant interrogation of Smt Indira Gandhi; perhaps the first time an Indian PM was in the dock. Questioned over a contradiction between a statement the PM had signed and her oral deposition, Smt Gandhi fumbled and the agile lawyer pounced on her and was able to get a ruling from Justice Jagmohan Lal Sinha that her evidence was not true in its entirety. Thundered Shanti Bhushan, "Can a person who was prepared to make incorrect statements be suitable to hold the office of the Prime Minister?" On the basis of Bhushan's deposition that she misused official machinery in her election campaign, Justice Sinha not only set aside Smt Gandhi's election but also disqualified her for six years. In a tribute to Justice Sinha, Justice Hidayatullah compared him to Justice Sirica of the Watergate case, whose judgment led the downfall of President Richard Nixon.

Of course, this earth-shaking judgment from the judge of a High Court against a powerful PM led to India's unfortunate and regrettable brush with dictatorship and its coarseness. As is well known, a nationwide agitation was launched against Smt Gandhi's continuation, followed by her declaration of Emergency.

Shanti Bhushan brought lustre to law by his vigorous espousal of the principles of law—irrespective of the personalities involved. He filed a habeas corpus case, which led to a regrettable Supreme Court order that the constitutionally mandated right to life was not sacrosanct, and during an Emergency there was no right to life or liberty and even if people were shot illegally, the courts could not intervene. Of course, one must not neglect to point out the controversial advice he gave to the Janata Party government to dismiss the legally constituted Congress governments in nine states after the Emergency for the only reason that they had no right to continue after Mrs Gandhi's ouster from power. This is undoubtedly one cross Bhushan continues to bear.

Bhushan has jumped to defend those accused of attacking the Parliament, identified himself with those responsible for the Delhi bomb blasts, and has even extended a helping hand to those who are followers of Maoists. He argues that he was concerned only with evidence and material on record and was not bothered by their anarchist aims.

However, Bhushan's struggle for defence of civil liberties, sustained campaign against corruption, and valiant efforts to bring accountability into administration of justice will always make his role in Indian legal history memorable. He will be remembered for his contribution to the political struggle for restoration of democracy.

In the narration of his life and work, the professional and the public meld gently. The author has a graceful style and is distinguished by gentle humour. One sample is furnished here. "Chief Justice Malik had constituted a bench with Justice Sapru to check whether Justice Sapru was sleeping. Lo and behold, after lunch, Justice Sapru was found sleeping. After the court rose, the Chief Justice told Justice Sapru that he had found him sleeping. Justice Sapru defended himself saying that he closed his eyes to concentrate better on arguments, and the Chief Justice had mistakenly thought that he had fallen asleep. The Chief Justice then asked Justice Sapru whether it was also necessary to snore for such concentration. The fact was that Justice Sapru not only slept but also snored loudly."

Somnath Chatterjee, the Lok Sabha speaker, while releasing this book, made the following observation, which sums up the achievements of this brilliant advocate. Said the speaker, "The book bears testimony to the tumultuous years of India's tryst with democracy. The memoir is not only biographical but also a chronicle of contemporary India. The book will be treated as an authentic source of information for researchers and the intelligentsia. The book is also a mirror of Shri Shanti Bhushan's endearing personality, his character, his conviction, his familial values and eventually a reflection of the finer sensitivity of his heart and mind."

This book will appeal to all interested in India's political and constitutional history. It will be a beacon to young legal aspirants when darkness seems to envelope both the bench and bar.

The book has 16 valuable appendices on important court cases like the judgment of the Supreme Court in Shaukat's habeas corpus petition as also the lawyer's tribute to Jawaharlal Nehru, Kamaraj and Justice Jagmohan Lal Sinha.

10 Sustainable Development

Academic Foundation deserves congratulations for bringing out a series of books released originally by the prestigious organisation Organisation for Economic Cooperation and Development (OECD). The OECD brings together the governments of countries committed to democracy and the market economy to tackle key economic, social and governmental challenges in the globalised world economy. It has 30 member countries, the economies of which account for 68 per cent of the world's trade and 88 per cent of the world's gross national income. The book under review is a part of four books of the 'Insight' series brought out by OECD, aimed at creating an informed debate on issues that affect our societies and economies.

It is an undeniable fact that populations of different countries continue to exploit resources available to them beyond their limits, in an environment whose ecological fragility makes it vulnerable to permanent destruction. The relationship of humans to environment has been one of give and take. When the rate of use overtakes the rate at which a resource can be replenished, then that resource will be drawn down and eventually disappear, affecting all the people, animals and plants that depend on it. The future of mankind is being shaped by issues that no single nation can tackle alone. Multilateral cooperation is instrumental in meeting the key challenges of this new world. 'Sustained Development'—the theme of this volume is

---

Tracey Strange and Anne Bayley; Academic Foundation; pp. 140; Price Rs 495/-

maintaining the maximum wellbeing over the long term. It helps in identifying and assessing our current situation, setting goals that will produce better results and making the right choices about the direction we have to take.

The book is divided into seven chapters, each dealing succinctly with problems connected with sustainable development. The first chapter defines what is sustainable development—a way of managing human impact on the world that leads to positive results for the greater benefit of human societies. The next chapter analyses the challenges posed by resource management, pollution control and climate phenomenon. The subsequent chapter emphasises planning for the future, what tools can help us to manage our systems for the long term. The crucial subject of how we behave as producers and consumers and its critical role is the problem tackled in the next chapter. How to measure the different aspects of sustainable development is analysed cogently. Accurate measurement and accounting of our natural, social and economic capital are essential to move forward on a sustainable path. The last chapter discusses how societies change and how technological innovation, changing consumption patterns and interaction of people, businesses, non-governmental organisations (NGOs) and government are the key factors leading to sustainable development.

A very useful part of the book is the copious short notes printed in boxes on relevant issues—to name a few—the RIO summit, the collapse of the Grand Banks cod fishery, mobile banking, melting glaciers, electronic waste , the rise of biofuels, etc. A valuable glossary of books to be read is appended. This is a seminal book bursting with ideas presented with crystal clarity, and must form compulsory reading for planners, social scientists and all concerned with saving this planet from doom.

BOOK REVIEWS »

11 The Unexplored Keynes

Anand Chandavarkar, unarguably, is the foremost exponent of the Indian economic scene and an acknowledged authority on John Maynard Keynes. He is noted for his grace in style, felicity of expression and profundity in knowledge. His credentials are impeccable. He is a graduate from the University of Bombay and the London School of Economics, where he was a student of Karl Popper and Michael Oakeshott, two political philosophers of world repute. Greater distinction is that he was the disciple of three Nobel laureates in economics—Friedrich Hayek, James Meade and Ronald Coase. One cannot have more distinguished teachers. Professionally, he served in Reserve Bank of India (RBI), International Monetary Fund (IMF), Organisation for Economic Cooperation and Development (OECD) and the World Bank. He is the author of 'Keynes and India' and 'Central Banking in Developed Countries'. His authoritative scholarship of Keynes ensured that he was invited as a speaker at the 10th Keynes seminar at the University of Kent, England. He has contributed to several learned journals.

Robert Skidelsky, author of the three-volume study of Keynes has brought out a couple of months ago a condensed version, 'Keynes: the Return of the Master', which has renewed the interest in this greatest economist of the 20th century. Chandavarkar's book is a valuable addition to Keynesiana, which is of absorbing interest. Keynes was

---

A.G. Chandavarkar; Academic Foundation; pp. 346; Price Rs 995/-

a man of the world: Cambridge don, investor, civil servant, member of the avant-garde Bloomsbury group and journalist. Keynes was the most creative and influential thinker of the last century.

The author had the fortune to be the last person to be given access to the Keynes' papers at King's college, Cambridge, prior to their closure for cataloguing. His archival pilgrimage has resulted in unearthing some gems in the life of Keynes. Chandavarkar, who has acquired international fame as an authority on Keynes with his book 'Keynes and India', has enhanced our knowledge of Keynes and thrown a flood of light on the great influence Keynes had on contemporary economists and the economic world. Keynes was a many-splendoured polymath and leading intellectual progenitor of the IMF.

One chapter deals with Keynes's role as a civil servant, his activities in the India office and the British treasury. He was awarded the title of the Companion of the Order of the Bath. He was adviser to three Chancellors of the Exchequer. He was member of a number of Commissions, one dealing with Indian currency and finance. His role in the formation of IMF was paramount. The author devotes one chapter to the nature of gold hoarding in underdeveloped countries and asserts that there should be mobilisation of gold hoards to cover part of the foreign exchange gap of the economy, required for the indispensable import content of the private sector, but through the mediation of government.

There is a succinct analysis of Keynes and central banking. Keynes's book 'Indian Currency and Finance' has been rightly accorded 'a permanent niche in the history of thought on central banking'. Keynes's originality extended far beyond an eclectic synthesis of central banking doctrine from English, European and US sources to an innovative adaptation to the Indian environment. Chandavarkar mourns the fact that Keynes was never called upon to advise on the establishment of the RBI. The author believes that Keynes's intellectual influence on development economics was indirect through the use made by others of the various testable and measurable concepts derived largely from the 'General Theory' and partly from the

'Treatise'. Keynes's views on the role of the state in India are relevant to all developing countries. The role in the context of privatisation, deregulation and liberalisation will alter, but not diminish, in both the transitional and the post-liberalisation phases. Chandavarkar devotes one chapter to analyse Keynes and the International Monetary System, and explains how the post-Keynesian developments in the structure and policies of the IMF in relation to the developing countries have gone beyond Keynes's International Clearing Union (ICU) provisions in major respects.

There is a very interesting analysis of Keynes as a social philosopher. Keynes ethical thinking was domesticated by G.E. Moore, and Edmund Burke was his most formative influence.

A subject of great interest is 'Was Keynes anti-Semitic?' Keynes was witheringly caustic about organised anti-Semitism. He had three acknowledged mentors—Alfred Marshall, Lionel Abrahams and Edwin Montagu—the last two were Jewish. Keynes never referred to them as Jewish. According to Chandavarkar, it is no exculpation of anti-Semitism to say that there are degrees and kinds of anti-Semitism. Keynes's attitudinal and selective anti-Semitism was certainly not of the monolithic variety like the rabid rancours of Ezra Pound and Richard Wagner. In retrospect, Keynes's anti-Semitism will be seen more as a peripheral fringe of an inherently compassionate personality, an unamiable foible rather than a fatal flaw of character, a blind spot which never blurred the totality of his social and political vision.

An example of Chandavarkar's omniscience is his informing us that in the Hindi film Chashm-e-Buddoor, the heroine is shown absorbed in Keynes' highly unreadable 'General Theory of Employment, Interest and Money'.

The second part of the book is a magnificent melange of masterly essays on a variety of topics. Chandavarkar has written eloquently about the need for 'refurbishing the case for an independent federal RBI'. He had earlier formulated a political economy agenda for the reconstitution of a constitutionally independent federal RBI. This article, which appeared in the 'Economic and Political Weekly' did not attract the attention of academics, and according to Chandavarkar, "the history of the RBI is a pathetic narrative of a Central Bank, which, ironically, was more assertive and independent in the British Raj, but has dwindled to a quasi-fiscal agency after independence with a consequent loss of status and influence. Currently, the office of the Governor is virtually a golden handshake franchise of the IAS fraternity". Stern indictment, indeed.

The next part has articles on four eminent persons, Dharma Kumar, I.G. Patel, Joan Robinson and Ralph Whitenack. Dharma Kumar was a distinguished economic historian and editor of the pioneering 'Cambridge Economic History of India': Volume 2, and we have a poignant portrait of this gracious lady with whom the author worked in RBI. Dharma Kumar invited Chandavarkar to contribute to the 'Cambridge Economic History of India'. Reviewing I.G. Patel's book 'Glimpses of Economic Policy' Chandavarkar provides a bird's-eye view of the attainments of I.G. Patel, who became the only Asian to become the Director of the prestigious London School of Economics. The author critically analyses Joan Robinson's 'Economic Philosophy' based on a memorial lecture and declares her work to be the testament of an agnostic, but more the affirmation of a high-minded social scientist and worthy of being described as an economic philosopher's handbook. The essay on 'Economics and Philosophy' is impressive and is a thoughtful reflection on economics and its relation to several disciplines. As regards the fourth personality, not many are familiar with the American adviser to the Sayajirao III, the Gaekwad of Baroda. Chandavarkar provides a lavish portrait of this economist from Wisconsin University, who played an eminent role in the foundation of the Bank of Baroda. The free wheeling Gujarati speaking Yankee was a natural who completely attuned to the ethos of Gujarati Baroda.

Dr Johnson wrote of Oliver Goldsmith, "Nothing did he touch that he did not leave unadorned." In a similar vein, whatever Chandavarkar touches he transforms into gold, and this book is yet one more example of his transmuting genius.

12 The Man Who Loved China

Simon Winchester is a British author and journalist who began as a geologist and worked on oil rigs in Africa. As a journalist he was kept prisoner by the Argentinean forces in the Falkland Islands. His book on the Oxford English dictionary, 'The Professor and the Madman' is a classic work in history. His other books 'A Crack in the Edge of the World', 'Krakatoa', and 'The Map that changed the World' were all on the *New York Times* best sellers list. Simon Winchester was made Officer of the Order of the British Empire by Queen Elizabeth in 2006.

The book under review, 'The Man Who Loved China', is about the British biochemist and Chinese scholar Joseph Needham. He was one of those rare persons who are so good at so many things that they astonish us. Cambridge educated in anatomy, physiology and chemistry, Needham became the West's leading authority on Chinese history. Needham 'succeeded, as few others are ever privileged to do, in making a significant and positive change to mankind's mutual understanding.'

A simple listing of the British professor's fascinations would fill pages and would include auto mechanics, irrigation, horticulture, public health, military and political science, and Chinese calligraphy. His stupendous work 'Science and Civilisation in China'—the product of 50 years of research and writing fills 23 huge volumes. His collaborators are completing five more.

Simon Winchester; Harper Collins; pp. 316; Price $27.95.

Winchester concentrates on Needham's flamboyant and eccentric character and those parts of his life that were filled with action, adventure and famous people. At Cambridge University, he pursued scientific research in biochemistry, and women with equal avidity. In 1924 he married Dorothy Moyle, another biochemist, and they maintained an open marriage, which lasted until her death more than 60 years later. In 1937, Needham took as his lover, Lu Gwei-Djen, a brilliant biochemist from Nanjing, and Moyle accepted her into their marriage. That arrangement too lasted until Moyle died, and Needham married Lu. She introduced Needham to China's language and culture at a time when Japan's invasion of the country focussed the West's attention and sympathy on the country.

Once Needham landed in China, he launched the research project that became the obsession that dominated the rest of his life—the discovery and recognition of China's many early technological achievements. His research began the day he arrived in the country and ended only with his death.

Most of the narrative, however, covers Needham's adventurous and dangerous three year stay in China during World War II. It was exciting times for him, filled with hardships, but he also met and befriended scientists, scholars, government and military leaders including Mao Zedong and Zhou Enlai. Both his work and these contacts gave him access for his research, and he found evidence everywhere of the early development of sophisticated technology.

Despite his support for the Chinese revolution, it was his passion for the country's past that captured him. As his research turned up early advances in Chinese science, Needham documented and made widely available to the rest of the world, the extraordinary accomplishments of an important culture.

Needham's life was a great deal more than scholarly. He was an explorer, adventurer, and womaniser whose wife and mistress remained friends for 50 years, while he carried on affairs with other women in other countries. He was a communist who never joined the party, but he nearly lost his academic standing when he was taken in by a scientific hoax, organised by leaders of the Soviet Union and designed to make it appear that the US had committed biological warfare during the Korean War.

The love affair between Joseph Needham and Lu Gwei-Djen propelled events that would change dramatically the western world's perceptions of China. As his mistress for life, she taught him the meticulous art of Chinese calligraphy. In studying her language, he fell in love with a country he had never seen. The outcome was the historical tome that Winchester regards, along with the Oxford English Dictionary, as one of the great intellectual achievements of all time.

Cambridge and the British diplomatic corps sent Needham to China to assess what the Chinese Universities needed, to pressure the Churchill government to provide it. It was the beginning of a lifelong quest to know everything about China and write it all down. For the rest of his life he worked 'all in the consequence of his love for a Chinese woman... to change the way the people of the West looked on the people of the East.' A puzzle often identified by historians as 'Needham's question' and central to much of his work is this: Why did China, having given the world its earliest understandings of the pure sciences, having invented printing, gunpowder, the wheelbarrow, the fishing reel, chain-pumps, the magnetic compass and hundreds of other practical devices at a pace 'unmatched by the World's other great civilisations including the Greeks' suddenly shut down in the 1500s? Why did this enormous country become isolated and xenophobic, just when modern science and industry began blooming in the West? Needham struggled with this mystery for decades, without a solution that suited him. According to Needham, the riddle is of less consequence these days. The more urgent need, Winchester writes for both himself and Needham, is to understand as much as possible of 'everything, good and ill, about the awe-inspiring, terrifying entity that is today's new China,' as it moves in the direction of world supremacy.

Needham was elected a Fellow of the Royal Society and the British Academy. Under the Royal Society's direction, Needham was the

Director of the Sino-British Science Cooperation Office in Chonquing from 1942 to 1946. Needham collaborated with the historian Wang Ling, who solidified Needham's passion for Chinese scientific history. After two years tenure as the first Head of the Natural Science division at United Nations Educational, Scientific and Cultural Organisation (UNESCO) in Paris—indeed, it was Needham who insisted that science should be included in the organisation's mandate—he returned to Gonville and Caius college in 1948, when Cambridge University partially funded his 'Science and Civilisation in China' series. He devoted much energy to the history of Chinese science until his retirement in 1990, even though he continued to teach biochemistry until 1966. He also supported the controversial Chinese communist claims of American biological warfare as an Inspector from 1952 to 1953 in North Korea. During the Korean War, he was banned by the American government from entering into American borders for 25 years. According to Simon Winchester, "Needham was intellectually in love with communism; and yet communist spymasters and agents, it turned out, had pitilessly duped him." (p. 212). Needham suffered from Parkinson's disease from 1982, and died at the age of 94 at his Cambridge home. In 2008, the Chair of Chinese in the University of Cambridge was endowed in honour of Joseph Needham.

Simon Winchester's book reads like a thriller and is as fascinating as the life of his hero. The eminent biochemist and Chinese scholar has been extraordinarily lucky to get a biographer whose work will be a unique account of a person and a country, both great achievers.

13 Dharavi: Documenting Informalities

This chronicle began as an attempt to tell the story of a specific informal settlement, a dwelling where people and buildings have been shaped by the necessities of a specific environment in a particular site. It aims at encouraging politicians and stakeholders to encourage development of Dharavi, providing infrastructure and services. However, by the time this book was released, Dharavi was embroiled in a master plan to sell off the entire area. Dharavi and its seven lakh residents were suddenly tossed in big international business schemes of powers far away from Dharavi. The Hollywood movie Slumdog Millionnaire made Dharavi world famous.

The book under review documents Dharavi using formal architectural methodologies. It showcases the issue of slums, the people who live there and their conditions. The initiative for this project came from the Royal University College of Fine Arts in Stockholm and the Swedish International Federation. The team that studied Dharavi included (apart from the two editors Maria Lantz and Jonathan Engquist) nine other established architects and planners, who visited Dharavi several times and held discussions with a large number of residents.

Dharavi is an unhealthy place with narrow alleys and overcrowded houses, where air and waterborne diseases are easily transmitted. It is swampy and wet with hazardous industries right next to where

---

Royal Institute of Fine Arts; Academic Foundation; pp. 303; Price Rs 1200/-

children play. Dharavi is an impossible place, a consequence of bad governance and sordid profiteering in a very ugly alliance. But this is not the whole truth. We have areas that are well established and developed. The distinguishing mark of Dharavi is 'production'. Some 80 per cent of the people are obtaining their income from some production or other. The largest areas of production are the leather industry, food preparation, pottery and textile work, other crafts and goldsmiths, bakeries, printers and production of a number of items, which have a global market. The recycling industry is predominant. Everything that can be remade, melted down or redistributed is used.

Dharavi is a tremendous proof of mankind's strength of will, ability, dignity and creativity. Family life is extremely congested in Dharavi. Neighbours and family members encroach on individual privacy. Crammed houses extend to space outside. Public area lies outside one's door. Children play in open spaces between structures. The sincerity of the contributors of this book is transparent in their exhaustive documentation to comprehend Dharavi and its mind-boggling life, its crooked lanes, businesses and people before it gets converted into a mighty residential and commercial complex. Local people have protested strongly against the grandiose plans of the government to transform Dharavi. This volume is a handsome tribute to the doughty residents of Dharavi. The team from Sweden has done a remarkable work.

The book has profuse illustrations and is a photographic record of the rapid changes taking place in Dharavi, transforming it into a global city. The writers have rendered a yeoman service to the residents of Dharavi. One only hopes that this book will open the eyes of the Government of Maharashtra and improve Dharavi, transforming it into an enviable part of Mumbai city and not allow it to languish in filth and garbage. Academic Foundation deserves congratulations on bringing out this edition, which is of great social significance.

BOOK REVIEWS »

14 Oprah: Kitty Kelley

Kitty Kelley is the female Boswell of the non-literary Johnsons of the 20th and 21st centuries. She has acquired fame for her biographies of Elizabeth Taylor, Jacqueline Kennedy, Frank Sinatra, the Bush dynasty and the Royalty of England. She has bagged several awards and her articles find place in leading journals of the world.

The book under review is an unauthorised biography of Oprah Winfrey—the undisputed queen of TV. How did Oprah—born in 1954 to an unwed teenage mother in racist Mississippi—become the richest and most influential woman of her generation? One clue is that she was aspirational from the very start. For the first few years of her life, she was raised largely by her grandparents. Her adolescence was deeply troubled. She was sexually abused. She was promiscuous. She even slept with men for money. Just before her 15th birthday, she gave birth to a premature baby, a son, who died a few weeks later. A week after giving birth she went back to school, where no one knew about her pregnancy.

Oprah, a black woman, believed 'excellence is the best deterrent to racism'. She spoke in local churches, scored in major speaking competitions and got herself elected vice-president of her mostly white high school. She was a pioneer being the first black woman on local TV. She was only 21. Her ambition was to emerge as the black

---

Crown Publishers; pp. 524; Price $ 30.

Barbara Walters. Sans doubt her success is due to her phenomenal ability to project warmth and authenticity. Her troubles with men, food and drugs make her seem vulnerable, but she never let her troubles submerge her. She was forever planning her breakthrough into major markets.

She was TV's highest-paid talk-show host by 33. She had around her people who were smart and utterly loyal to her and worked like dogs. By 50, as confidently predicted by her, she was a billionaire. The queen of confessional TV has always campaigned for liberal social values and believes in reading books. She has been harassed for years by those who want to make money off their relationship with her—ex-boyfriends, disgruntled employees and the like. Today, everyone who works for her must sign an elaborate confidentiality agreement pledging not to talk about her—ever.

Oprah has probably had more impact on popular culture than any other single figure of our time. Sinners as various as Mike Tyson and Bill Clinton come forward on bended knees, receive her blessings and go back into the world, shining like new money. Tears are undoubtedly Winfrey's *lingua franca*. From the start she gauged the value of victims, but she was conscious that she has to heal not just her guests but her audience. Decades before Barack Obama, Oprah Winfrey led to a post-racial America, simply by gazing into her predominantly white audience without a touch of bitterness. Kelley's biography is a bare-it-all type of biography and is full of innuendos and invectives. But she is eminently readable and has done her research meticulously.

15 A Masterful Spirit: Homi Bhabha

There are few biographies of the 'Father of India's Nuclear Revolution' —Dr Homi Bhabha. This lacuna is admirably filled by this book by Indira Chowdhury and Ananya Dasgupta, both closely associated with the Tata Institute of Fundamental Research (TIFR) archives. Chowdhury holds the New India Fellowship to write the institutional history of TIFR and is the recipient of the Tagore prize in 2001 for her book 'The Frail Hero and Virile History.' Dasgupta also conceptualised the Bhabha centenary permanent exhibition.

The book is profusely illustrated with rare photographs of Bhabha, his family, his great acquaintances, his sketches of eminent scientists, his paintings and correspondence. Also there are delightful doodles by him. This biography recapitulates Bhabha's birth, childhood in Malabar hill, Cathedral High School, Elphinstone College, Royal Institute of Science, Cambridge, the romance with physics, doctoral thesis on cosmic radiation, Indian Institute of Science with C.V. Raman, the establishment of the Atomic Energy Commission and finally, the Atomic Research Centre, which eventually became BARC. Commending him for admission to Fellow of the Royal Society, C.V. Raman and a galaxy of distinguished scientists wrote "Bhabha is a distinguished Mathematical physicist. He has contributed notably to our understanding of cosmic ray phenomenon, especially the absorption of the rays, the origin of electronic showers."

Indira Chowdhury and Ananya Dasgupta; Penguin; pp. 240; Price Rs 1299/-

Bhabha was a multifaceted personality. Basically a scientist, he played a violin in a philharmonic concert, and took part in the Cambridge regatta. He sketched the organ players, prepared the cover of the 'Caian'—his college magazine. He designed the sets for a performance of a Spanish play 'Life is a Dream' as also the sets of Mozart's 'Idomeno' for the Cambridge musical society.

There are three outstanding chapters—embellished by photographs —dealing with Bhabha and J.R.D. Tata, Bhabha and Jawaharlal Nehru and the establishment of the TIFR. Bhabha's vision and ability to transform it to reality emerge clearly from these chapters.

Vikram Sarabhai in a tribute said, "Bhabha is a perfect example of the opposite of what C.P. Snow refers to as the alienation of scientists and humanists. He represented the best in the modern educated world and the best of science, of the arts. Bhabha not just understood the language of modern science. He was equally thrilled with a recital of bharatanatyam or a beautiful bronze from a temple." C.V. Raman wrote of him, "...he is the modern equivalent of Leonardo da Vinci."

The authors deserve special kudos for their skilful choice of photos, significant letters to eminent scientists by Bhabha and their responses. We have charming photographs of Bhabha with Albert Einstein, J.R.D. Tata and Jawaharlal Nehru, and delightful cartoons of R.K. Laxman. The volume scales new technical heights. The layout and arrangement of images makes the volume highly impressive.

This is one of the finest books on a giant in science and lover of arts and is a must read for all students of science as also administrators of scientific organisations. It is undoubtedly a collector's item.

16 Clint: A Retrospective

Clint Eastwood is 80 and this coffee-table book is a rich tribute to this legend from Hollywood on his 60 years of achievement, both in front and behind the camera. Richard Schickel himself is an award winning documentary film maker and distinguished biographer of Charlie Chaplin, Woody Allen and Marlon Brando. A bonus DVD features a biography of Clint directed by Schickel with clips from 35 films in 35 years of association with Warner brothers.

In an introduction, Eastwood states that he is a 'genre' movie maker and that made possible creating variations of a basic theme, a chance to refresh a film in question, making it new for the audience and the director. Clint truly began his career in the spaghetti western A Fistful of Dollars and he is the guy who drifts into town, encounters ordinary people oppressed by some kind of evil from which he delivers them and thereafter, departs without explanation.

His directorial debut was the scary Play Misty for Me, a dark study of male sexual carelessness and female revenge. He became a force to be reckoned with. Dirty Harry made him a super star. He went on to become director and we have some great movies—Mystic River, Million Dollar Baby, Letters from Iwo Jima, and Gran Torino. Clint Eastwood is a Hollywood icon who has carved out a successful career of 60 years and 60 movies. Acclaimed for acting, directing and for

---

Richard Schickel; Sterling; pp. 288; Price Rs 1499/-.

his musical compositions, he has won several Oscars and is a true cinematic great.

Clint began with Rawhide—a Western TV series that ran for seven years and 217 episodes. A giant leap was from Rawhide to A Fistful of Dollars—a Sergio Leone spaghetti Western, followed by For a Few Dollars More and The Good, Bad and the Ugly. Recent classics by him are Mystic River, Bridges of Madison County and Invictus—the last being on Nelson Mandela. The production and critical reception of Eastwood's most important films are recounted in this book in detail; especially outstanding is Schickel's analysis of the still controversial Dirty Harry. Schickel zeroes in on Eastwood's appeal, showing through his acute interpretive readings of the films, how the actor combines the masculine authority and repressed rage of Gary Cooper and John Wayne with an almost postmodern ironic self-consciousness.

Time and Life film critic for 43 years, Schickel penned a substantive biography in 1997. What is impressive is his intimate familiarity with Eastwood and his work. He has known the star for 33 years and in an introduction, reviews the career and recalls personal moments with Eastwood. A film-by-film account of his oeuvre follows, from the mid-1960s Italian spaghetti westerns and his breakthrough in Dirty Harry to his recent, commercially bold treatments of race relations, Gran Torino and Invictus. Schickel assesses each movie with acute insight. Over 300 spectacular images, including dynamic stills from memorable screen performances and revealing behind-the-scenes photos, are accompanied by Richard Schickel's incisive and illuminating commentary.

This is a wonderfully well written and illustrated book providing commentary that will have you admiring Clint for his achievements.

BOOK REVIEWS »

17 Kashmir Crisis: Unholy Anglo–Pak Nexus

Solid research and lucid style are the highlights of this book. The author Dr Saroja Sundararajan held posts of Principal in several colleges in South India and authored 11 books including two celebrated biographies—those of S. Satyamurty and C.P. Ramaswami Iyer. She has bagged several awards for academic excellence.

Kashmir is 'a riddle wrapped in a mystery inside an enigma' and the author has successfully unravelled the mystery. The core of the book is the history of the crisis from 1947 to 1971 and brings out clearly, the role of Perfidious Albion—its bias against India and the betrayal of India's trust by the British government and their minions including Lord Mountbatten. We have a history of Hindu Kashmir, its role in cultural integration of India, and the forcible conversion of Hindus to Islam from the 14th to the mid-19th century. By then Kashmir had become a Muslim majority state. The accession of the state to India in October 1947 led to a series of disastrous events. Britain throughout played a partisan role siding with Pakistan. The UN Security Council was under the influence of the western powers who branded India as an aggressor.

The British called the Indians 'natives' and believed in the superiority of western civilisation and failed to comprehend Indian society. The establishment of the Indian National Congress in 1885 led to the

---

Dr Saroja Sundararajan; Kalpaz Publications; pp. 421; Price Rs 850/-.

British government creating a hiatus between Hindus and Muslims. The partition of India was the pinnacle of British achievement, which ensured Pakistan's hostility. Britain adopted an attitude of 'unmixed malice' towards India after 1947. British army officers serving in Pakistan tried to nullify the painstaking efforts of India to solve the dispute. Zaffrullah Khan and Bhutto spewed venom on India during discussions in the Security Council. Britain ignored Pakistan's illegal annexation of Indian territories and the Azad Kashmir.

Pakistan signed the Simla agreement, and between 1972 and till the Kargil war, there was no major conflict. Pakistan enacted a treacherous drama while a goodwill bus *yatra* was undertaken—26 Hindus were done to death by militants in Kashmir. Pakistan began sending her troops in the guise of Mujahideens to launch the Kargil war.

The author says that British documents refer to the dissatisfaction of some Indian leaders with the policy of Nehru on Kashmir. The costliest blunder was to take away Kashmir from the charge of Vallabhbhai Patel, who held the crucial portfolios of Home and States. Patel was a talented administrator, who accomplished easily the Herculean task of integrating the 562 princely Indian states. If only he had a free hand in Kashmir, the situation would have been in our favour.

The author provides a succinct analysis of the various missions of Dixon, Graham, Jarring, who visited the sub-continent. The author's solution to Kashmir problem lies in Pakistan and India uniting, though 'It may take a century or more for this to happen, but a century is not a long period in the life of a nation as ancient as India'. This is an empty dream dealing with such a recalcitrant enemy as Pakistan.

BOOK REVIEWS »

18 India's Great Masters

When the definitive history of photography comes to be written, Raghu Rai, India's best known photographer, will capture an important place. In this book, he has caught India's masters in music in concerts, in their homes, amidst their *gurus*, and in distinct locations. He profiles only 13 masters and they are Ravi Shankar, Ali Akbar Khan, M.S. Subbulakshmi, Mallikarjun Mansur, Kumar Gandharva, S. Balchander, Alla Rakha, Zakir Hussain, Vilayat Khan, Bismillah Khan, Kishori Amonkar, Hariprasad Chaurasia and Bhimsen Joshi. Some of these masters have departed and their portraits form an invaluable record of Indian musical heritage.

Rai has covered many social, political and cultural themes, and his photo essays have appeared in *Time, Life, National Geographic* and *the New York Times*. He has also to his credit a number of books, including 'The Sikhs', 'Calcutta', 'Taj Mahal', 'India' and 'Mother Teresa'.

A vital part of this book is the illuminating text written by noted writer and music expert Ashok Vajpeyi, Chairman of Lalit Kala Akademi. His profiles of these musicians reveal highlights of their life and what makes them tick. He provides us remarkable snapshots of their lives, couched in lyrical language.

We have chosen only 5 of the 13 musicians covered in this book. Ravi Shankar remains a legend of our times—combining in his

---

Raghu Rai and Ashok Vajpeyi; Harper Collins; pp. 167; Price Rs 3500/-

person and his music, the deeply classical and the firmly modern. A world renowned sitar player, Ravi Shankar introduced the world to the riches of Indian classical music. Ustad Allauddin Khan taught various instruments, including the sitar, the violin, the flute, and his disciples—Ravi Shankar, Pannalal Ghosh, Ustad Ali Akbar Khan and Nikhil Banerjee grew into major musicians. Yehudi Menuhin termed Ravi Shankar "without doubt one of the greatest musicians today. He has not only brought Indian classical music to the West, but he has also, in no small degree, influenced Western music...his genius and humanity can only be compared to that of Mozart's." Rich tribute from a great violinist and highly deserved! Coming to India's Queen of music, M.S. Subbulakshmi—it is written that the gold of her voice glittered more than the jewels she had around her neck and on her fingers. A sense of magic pervaded her—magic created by her voice with such simplicity and humility. Her music was utterly pure and it purified the listeners as well. There are many words that acquire a depth of meaning, a glow of relevance when they are used to describe the music of M.S.—grace, transparency, purity by any standards. Whether of skill or vision, of craft or economy, this was high music, lofty, noble, pure, well-structured, glowing inwardly and outwardly. Mahatma Gandhi impressed both by the music and the *bhakti* of M.S. had said, "She loses herself in *bhajans*. To sing bhajans is one thing, to sing it by losing oneself in God is quite different." M.S. sang *bhajans* of Meera, Tulsidas, Surdas, Kabir and Guru Nanak. She was distinguished by the quality of her voice, spiritual fervour and high creativity of interpretation. Life and music were not different for M.S.—life was her music and music was her life.

To Bismillah Khan goes the credit of transforming a folk music instrument into a worthy vehicle of classical music. He made the *shehnai* popular on the classic concert platform and became one of the most sought-after classical instrumentalists of our times. Bismillah's music had Kashi's fragrance and the abandon of Ganga. Like the holy city and the holy river, his music appears eternal, ceaseless and ever-flowing. He would claim with genuine conviction that a person 'who lives in Kashi lives in heaven.' The Ustad had vigorous training in Varanasi from his uncle Ali Baksh Khan. He was so humble that he believed that like his own instrument, he was a mere instrument of divine powers. A devout Muslim, he played the *shehnai* at the famous Vishwanath temple in Varanasi. The *shehnai* was practised and mastered by Muslims, but was played in Hindu temples. His pristine classicism was more inclusive than usual. It included *chaiti*, *kajri* and *jhoola*, semi-classical forms noted for earthiness and sensuousness.

Our next artist is Kishori Amonkar whose music is full of contradictions. She has a deep respect for tradition and values of classicism. Her aim was originality. She received training in the Jaipur Atrauli Gharana. Her music incorporates elements from elsewhere—not from any *gharanas,* but from her own thinking and creatively bold personality. Mohan Nadkarni described her as one of two musicians who pioneered the avant-garde movement in Hindustani music. In her *parampara* is *prayogdharma*, that is, her music tradition lives through experiments. She conveys eloquently diverse emotions—separation, longing, waiting, eagerness, anxiety and tension. One notes her efforts to identify with nature. Kishori's music reaches out to the primeval elements of nature.

Our last musician is S. Balchander, who is among the exceptions in being a major musician from outside the more dominant and age-old *guru-sishya parampara*. He went on mastering one instrument after another, entirely on his own, untutored sans a *guru*. He started playing well on the tabla, the harmonium, the *bul-bul thara*, the *mridangam*, the *dilruba* and the sitar. The *veena* attracted him and he devoted his whole time to it and evolved a new style and a new school of playing the *veena*. He composed orchestral music for All India Radio (AIR) that was admired for its rare beauty and variety. He was one of the few South Indian musicians well-versed in and knowledgeable about North Indian and Western classical music. In his last years, he got embroiled in a slanging match with Semmangudi Sreenivasa Iyer on Maharaja Swathi Thirunal. Balchander believed that the Maharaja did not compose a single note. He even denied the existence of the

Maharaja. It was widely believed that Balchander was wasting time, energy and attention on a non-issue.

The book under review is a photographic journey into the heart of classical music and one great photographer's tribute to the great exponents of Indian classical music. Most of the photographs have captured the essence of the artists with both beauty and fidelity. One cannot conceive of a better way of paying tribute to these great Indian classical masters. Beyond doubt, this is fulfillment of a collector's dream.

19 Raja Ravi Varma: Painter of Colonial India

The Governor of Maharashtra—Shri K. Sankaranarayanan, releasing the book under review said that Raja Ravi Varma was a rare phenomenon to have happened to the world of art and it was he who brought Indian paintings on the world canvas, gave 'face' to many Gods and Goddesses in the Hindu pantheon. If there was ever a painter who could claim to have completely changed the way popular Indian imagination pictured its Gods, Goddesses, myths and legends, then it was that charismatic Keralite Raja Ravi Varma.

This book by Rupika Chawla is an account of the painter from a royal family in the background of colonial India, and the impact of this milieu on his profession as an aristocratic itinerant painter. This lavishly illustrated book is a great collection of paintings from royal and private collections and museums, and works hitherto unseen, along with previously undisclosed maps, letters, photographs and other archival material.

For this magnificent coffee-table book, Chawla has travelled all over the country for many years, prising out the slightest of secrets. This book offers fresh insights, especially into the way he painted, obtained from the diary of the Raja of Aundh (near Pune), in whose court the prince-painter spent a lot of time painting. The Raja was a very

Rupika Chawla; Mapin; pp. 360; Price Rs 3950/-.

careful observer and genuine questioner. To quote the author, "he writes about the way Raja Ravi Varma painted, the hours he painted and about the time and trouble he took to get emotion on the faces he made, reworking them several times...He also writes about the painter's fascination for the nine yard *sari* because it showed the body so well." Chawla portrays the times the painter lived in. She shows us how this modern man with a vision was able to use turn-of-the-century technological innovations such as electricity, the railways, newspapers and oleographs.

The author, who is the wife of the ex-Chief Election Commissioner Navin Chawla, is a conservator of paintings based in Delhi, has restored several Ravi Varma's paintings at her studio and also gives training in conservation. Together with artist A. Ramachandran, she organised the seminal exhibition on Raja Ravi Varma in 1993 at the National Museum, Delhi, which brought about a strong revival of the artist and his work. This well-researched book traces the sources used by Ravi Varma, examines the techniques and methodology of his paintings, discusses their conservation and the problem of fakes and copies, and is a goldmine for historians, collectors, curators and art lovers.

Rupika Chawla revealed how she was fascinated by the Kerala painter and spent over two decades tracing his life, locating lost paintings, and interviewing descendants of his family members, friends and acquaintances. This book provides a peek into the artist's inner world, his muses, visits to different parts of the country and the influences in his work.

The author declared that very little was known about this painter. Who was he? How was he able to make the kind of paintings he made, what motivated him, what was his background, the times he lived in, who were the people he knew, his collectors, the value of his art—then and now, his technique and method of painting, the people who were influenced by him and the value of his art today. In her research, all these questions were answered, and much more. Her favourite paintings were the Mysore collection. They were among the last that Ravi Varma did. In terms of composition, they are complex, well executed and exquisitely beautiful, while also concentrating and expressing the drama that involves their narrative. Ravi Varma balanced tradition and modernity, combined business enterprise with his love of painting, understood the commercial value of art and was a forerunner in propagating art. With that in mind, he started the oleograph press and wished to make a museum, but died before he could manage that.

Raja Ravi Varma was born on April 29, 1848, in Kilimanoor, Kerala. He belonged to a family of scholars, poets and artists. Noted in his family were Vidwan Koil Tampuran, author of the famous Kathakali work 'Ravana Vijayam'; Raja Raja Varma, who painted after the Tanjore style, and Uma Amba Bai Tampuratty who composed 'Parvati Swayamvaram', a work for the *thullal* dance. As a small boy, he filled the walls of his home with pictures of animals, acts and scenes from his daily life, which impressed his uncle, Raja Raja Varma as the signs of a blossoming genius. The uncle not only gave the first drawing lessons to his nephew, but took a keen interest in his further training and education with the help of the ruling king, Ayilyam Thirunal. When he was only 14, Ravi Varma was sent to Thiruvananthapuram where he stayed in the Kilimanoor palace and was taught water painting by the palace painter Ramaswami Naidu. Here Varma's talent was nurtured by the personal interest of the King, who exposed him to the famous paintings of Italian painters. Ravi Varma had been using the indigenous paints made from leaves, flowers, tree bark and soil, which his uncle Raja Raja Varma prepared for him. His first set of oil paints was brought from Madras after noticing a newspaper advertisement.

Rupika Chawla has done detection of an extraordinary type for this book on the life and times of Raja Ravi Varma, considered by many to be India's first modern painter. She has given us the portrait of 'a man in full' by doggedly following the most evanescent of clues across India, ferreting out unknown Ravi Varma's paintings, digging into dispersed archives, studying scores of his work, tracing his scattered descendants in pursuit of bits of information or some forgotten and damaged Ravi Varma canvas—even making the slightest of links lead into fascinating revelations.

The readers are taken on a journey and we can almost visualise the painter prince's life unfold before us, and Chawla draws for us a picture of his artistic struggles. We also learn more about his models and muses. The author has effectively used the diaries of his younger brother C. Raja Raja Varma—they worked and travelled together on commissions. A man ahead of his times, he was a marketing genius and shrewd entrepreneur. He set up the Ravi Varma Fine Arts Lithographic Press to make his art more accessible, to travel far beyond the circle of wealthy patrons. Not satisfied with the quality of the prints in India, he dispatched a man to Germany in 1893 to find an expert chromo-lithograph printer, who could help them produce superior Indian-made oleographs. The young German Fritz Schleicher came to India and became the printer and manager of the oleograph and chromo-lithograph workshop. Chawla tracked down Schleicher's grandson, Robert Sandhu, to garner fascinating details about the collaboration between Schleicher and the Varma brothers.

Till Ravi Varma arrived on the scene, Indian art was wondrous, metaphoric, symbolic, abstract, geometric and much more, but never directly representational of the retinal reality. Most importantly, Hindu Gods were not perceived to be made in the image of man. They were portrayed by the depiction of their attributes in hundreds of different styles and manners. But the setting up of the Ravi Varma Press in 1894 in Bombay changed all that. Soon, from Simla to Trivandrum and from Calcutta to Bombay, every middle-class Hindu home in the 20th century was and is decorated with highly affordable prints of Ravi Varma's 'natural and realistic' renderings of Lakshmi, Saraswati, Rama, Sita and Hanuman, to name just a few. Moreover, Ravi Varma's penchant for the dramatic pageant influenced popular theatre and films, thereby increasing the impact of his artifice manifold.

In the latter half of the 19th century, the medium of oil on canvas that was Ravi Varma's chosen style of painting European realism (though outmoded in Europe by then)—was still unfamiliar and novel in India. But once Ravi Varma had mastered both his technique and his style around the 1870s, there was no stopping him. His familial links with the Travancore ruling family ensured a network of connections that led to a spate of commissions ranging from tiny states like Pudukottai, Aundh and Bhavnagar to big ones like Mysore, Baroda and Hyderabad. He was much sought after not only for his portraits, but also for his 'thematic' paintings depicting pivotal scenes from Hindu myths and Sanskrit literature.

Paradoxically, in contrast to his immense mass appeal and popular influence as India's first painter of iconic images, the life and legacy of Ravi Varma had never been seriously studied till now. This volume, which admirably fills a gap, is not a heavy academic tome. In style and substance, it is hugely engaging, carrying its scholarship with a remarkable lightness of grace. Chawla's chronicling of Ravi Varma's life and works is full of anecdotes from secondary sources such as accounts of his patrons, colleagues and friends, the most important among these being the diaries kept by his beloved brother C. Raja Raja Varma, who was his pupil and partner in virtually all of the commissions and enterprises that Ravi Varma undertook.

What makes this book significantly different is that it covers brilliantly social, cultural and political life in colonial India—especially that of the native princes, and attempts to underline the newly emerging dynamic link between technology and a colonised society bound by moribund feudal values that was aspiring to modernity, freedom and democracy. So the 'shortening of time and distances' by the coming of the Railways, the place of art 'in the time of mechanical reproduction' and the double-edged politics of cultural nationalism all come into focus in this absorbing narrative of a painterly transience.

20 Mint Road Milestones

April 2009 to March 2010 was the platinum jubilee (PJ) year of the Reserve Bank of India (RBI), which commenced operations on April 1, 1935. The RBI has rightly celebrated the entire year with a variety of events such as release of PJ stamps, release of special PJ coins, outreach programmes at schools, colleges and villages, lectures by eminent persons, discussions, etc. One of these worthy of high praise is their bringing out 'Mint Road Milestones' a coffee-table book—a copiously illustrated history of the RBI. The bank has earlier released three volumes of history of RBI with exhaustive and exhausting reading material aimed at the student and the scholar.

Governor Dr Subbarao in a foreword to the book under review declares, "The Bank has been at the forefront of building public policy and economic thought. Its story, in some ways reflects the story of finance and banking in India...this retrospective gives a glimpse into the bank's eventful past and the road it has traversed. The journey is supported by visuals and vignettes that transcend time to bring alive the spirit of one of the oldest central banks of the developing world."

An introductory chapter furnishes a cogent and abbreviated history of the bank, beginning with the Hilton Young Commission, the efforts of J.M. Keynes, the Central Banking Enquiry Committee Report, etc. The RBI Act came into force on January 1, 1935. The first governor

---

Bazil Sheikh, Ranjeeta Dubey and Surendra Khot; Reserve Bank of India; pp. 476; Price Rs 1750/-.

was Sir Osborne Smith, an Australian who resigned before his term was over. We are furnished with details of how RBI was transformed from a private shareholders bank to a fully government owned institution. The slow, sure and steady enlargement of its functions led to new areas as agriculture, industry, economic development and financial inclusion. Covered are the devaluation of the rupee, demonetisation of high-value currency notes, exchange control regulations, establishment of several bodies such as Unit Trust of India (UTI), Industrial Development Bank of India (IDBI), Agriculture Research and Development Centre (ARDC), etc. All these innovations were in addition to the traditional role of issue of currency, debt management, etc. A primary concern of the Bank was the building up of a tremendous database with a variety of publications like the Annual Report, the Currency and Finance Report and the valuable monthly bulletins. The bank provides a cornucopia of valuable information on vital aspects of our economy.

The period of 75 years is divided, in this volume, into six phases. The first period (1935-1949) covers the years up to nationalisation of RBI and the legislation—Banking Companies Act. The first era of planning (1950-1968) forms the essence of the next section and includes establishment of new institutions to build a new financial architecture for the country. The crucial event of bank nationalisation and its aftermath is the subject matter of the third period (1969-1981), which was plagued by a nightmarish external payments position and witnessed our resort to International Monetary Fund (IMF) loan. The period (1982-1990) was the era of liberalisation, especially after mid-1980s. The year 1991 spelt crisis and became the stage for jumping into opening up of the economy toward a market economy. It covered the years 1991-2000. The final phase is dedicated to the new millennium (2001-2009) and shows how reforms were consolidated and the country moved over to strikingly higher growth rates.

A timeline of events very skilfully summarises major world events throughout the volume. International events of significance are provided in a capsule form. This includes not merely banking developments, but other arenas too. A few examples will illustrate the gamut of this successful attempt. 'Black Tuesday' when the US Stock Exchange collapsed (1929), the Royal Indian Naval Mutiny (1946), Bandung Conference (1955), launching of Sputnik (1957), Martin Luther King's outstanding oration— 'I Have A Dream' (1963), Mother Teresa being awarded the Nobel Prize and the Bharat Ratna (1997 and 1980), Barack Obama becoming America's first-ever black president (2009). All the Nobel laureates in economics are covered with their photographs. This work of highlighting major events is meticulously done and is highly commendable.

The RBI, as stated earlier, has published three volumes of its authorised history covering the period up to 1981. These are serious tomes for the scholars and students. The volume under review will attract not only students but the lay public—the vast number of persons thirsting to improve their knowledge and widen their vision.

There are three chapters worthy of special mention. One is devoted to all the 22 governors beginning with Sir Osborne Smith to the latest incumbent Dr D. Subbarao. One paragraph is allotted to each governor, recounting the highlights of his tenure. We have excellent portraits of all the governors. Another chapter deals with all the buildings owned by the bank at various centres including the three training colleges in Mumbai, Chennai and Pune. There is a hilarious account of the statues of the Yaksha and the Yakshini on the two sides of the entrance to the RBI, New Delhi office building. Questions were raised in Parliament about the Yaksha and the Yakshini. The Yaksha bore an uncanny resemblance to a Bombay politician Sadobha Patil. Actually the statue is that of Kuber, the God of wealth. The Yakshini, which was described as the statue of a semi-naked woman is the representation of agriculture and prosperity. The chapter 'Lives and Times at the Bank' will surely make the reader nostalgic with rare and unobtainable photos of persons, groups and events during this long period. Special mention must be made of the inclusion of the photo of Subedar Sam Bahadur who worked with several governors and who came in for special praise by Governor H.V.R. Iengar, who paid tribute to Sam Bahadur's *dharma*.

The Governor and his team of editors deserve to be warmly complimented in bringing out this excellent compendium, which is an easy-to-absorb capsule history of the Indian economy for 75 years with a backdrop of international events. It is a veritable feast to the eyes and a rich repast to the brain.

21 Shakespeare

An impressive series of biographies edited by James Atlas include Muhammad by Karen Armstrong, Thomas Jefferson by Christopher Hitchens and Beethoven by Edmund Morris. The latest in this series is Shakespeare by Bill Bryson. Bryson is, of course, the well-known author of 'A Short History of Nearly Everything', which was shortlisted for the Samuel Johnson Prize, bagged the Aventis Prize for science books in 2004 and was also awarded the Descartes Prize in 2005. Bryson's last book was the semi-autobiographical hilarious 'The Life and Times of the Thunderbolt Kid'.

The book under review is a biography of William Shakespeare, which will cause several eyebrows to be raised. Since there are thousands of books on the Bard of Avon—why one more? Reading the volume will make one realise that biographies of Shakespeare have so far been based on a jungle of wild speculation based on negligible, unverified facts.

Bill Bryson has waded through the entire Shakespeare-iana, sifted and recorded episodes in his research with considerable wit and commendable vigour. The biography is at once a vivid, fast paced work that encompasses every facet of the Bard's life and times.

Bill Bryson; Harper Collins; pp. 200; Price Rs 325/-.

Facts unavailable hitherto tumble out of this cornucopia, and a few are culled out and given for the entertainment and education of the reader.

Scholars have counted every word Shakespeare wrote, logged every dib and jot. Shakespeare's works contain 138,198 commas, 26,794 colons, and 15,785 question marks; ears are spoken of 401 times in his plays; his characters refer to 'love' 2,259 times but to 'hate' only 183 times; altogether he left us 888,647 words, made up of 31,959 speeches, spread over 118,406 lines.

Much is made of Shakespeare's learning—he knew as much as a lawyer, doctor or statesman or accomplished professional of his age. He is supposed to have deduced the orbital motions of heavenly bodies well before any astronomer did. Shakespeare was made into a committee of talents. His vocabulary showed a more than usual interest in medicine, law, military affairs and natural history. He mentions 180 plants and employs 200 legal terms. However, Bryson proves that Shakespeare's knowledge was not all that distinguished. He gets his geography wrong. He puts a sail—maker in Bergamo—the most landlocked city in Italy. If he knew Venice had canals, he gave no hint of it in the plays he set there. Ancient Egyptians played billiards. Caesar's Rome has clock—the first one ticked 1400 years later. Whatever his other virtues, Shakespeare was not conspicuously worldly.

Shakespeare's real gift was as a phrase maker. Many of his phrases have entered the common language. Among them: one fell swoop, vanish into thin air, bag and baggage, play fast and loose, go down the primrose path, be in a pickle, budge an inch, the milk of human kindness, more sinned against than sinning, remembrance of things past, beggar all description, cold comfort, more in sorrow than in anger, tower of strength, foregone conclusion.

If we take the Oxford Dictionary of Quotations, then roughly one-tenth of all the most quotable utterances in English are from Shakespeare—an impressive proportion, indeed.

Shakespeare's plays might have been lost except for the efforts of his close friends, John Hemminges and Henry Condell, who brought out a folio edition of his complete works. It contained 18 plays. The great repository of the first folio today is a modest building two blocks away from the Capitol Hill in Washington DC—the Folger Shakespearean Library.

Mention must be made of the ludicrous attempt of P.T. Barnum of 'Barnum and Bailey Circus' fame, who tried shipping to USA the birthplace of Shakespeare, placing it on wheels and sending it on a perpetual tour round the country—a prospect so alarming that money was swiftly raised in Britain, through a committee headed by Charles Dickens, to save the house as a museum and shrine. This reviewer had a chance to pay homage to Shakespeare at his birthplace, and was deeply moved by the impressive manner in which it is preserved for posterity.

Lytton Strachey wrote, "The first duty of a biographer is to preserve a becoming brevity, which excludes everything that is redundant and nothing that is significant." Strachey who evolved a new genre of biographical writing could not have had a better disciple than Bill Bryson. Bill Bryson's book is a *tour-de-force* and worth reading and rereading many times. It is pure nectar.

22 The Art of Costume Designing

Who can forget the bewitching angels Vyjayanthimala in Amrapali and Waheeda Rehman in Guide—both in costumes inspired by classical sculptures? Vyjayanthimala adorned in her role as Amrapali swept all of their feet by the vibrant costume inspired by Ajanta and complemented by an artistic hairdo and ornate jewellery. Who created this magic? Bhanu Athaiya.

Richard Attenborough, celebrated producer of Gandhi in an affectionate foreword to the book under review writes, "Bhanu Athaiya is the revered doyenne of Indian costume designers... For the benefit of future generations of film makers, film lovers and designers, it is important to landmark the work done by someone with a such knowledge, vision and passion." He wrote that while it took him 17 long years to set up Gandhi, his dream film, it took him just 15 minutes to make up his mind that Bhanu Athaiya was the right person to create the many hundreds of Indian costumes that the film required.

She was the first Indian to bag the Oscar for her work in Attenborough's Gandhi. She annexed the Lifetime Achievement Award at the South Asian International Festival in 2005, as also the Filmfare Lifetime Achievement Award in 2009. Her work has been displayed in the

---

Bhanu Athaiya; Collins; pp. 188; Price Rs 2500/-.

Festival of India, New York. She bagged two National Awards for costume designing for Lekin and Lagaan.

Athaiya hails from Kolhapur, where her forefather's book 'Rukmini Swayamwar' was prescribed as Sanskrit reading in the Rajaram College of Kolhapur University. It is revealing to note that the prize she won for the best essay—a princely amount of Rs 30 was spent on viewing seven times, Walt Disney's Fantasia, famous for its waltz of flowers.

Bhanu comes from a privileged family—her father was a man of leisure, indulging his artistic passions and interests while encouraging his large family of a wife and seven children to do the same. It was this encouragement that led Bhanu out of her sprawling house in Kolhapur to the city of Bombay, in order to pursue her passion—studying art at the J.J. School of Arts. "Travelling to Bombay was very exciting for me. It had been a dream for a long time, and I felt like it was finally happening. I made the journey with my art teacher from Kolhapur, who had convinced my mother to send me," recalls Bhanu. She annexed a gold medal from the J.J. School of Arts. She secured a French government scholarship and went to Paris to study art, culture and cinema.

The next milestone in Bhanu's life was her job at a magazine called 'Eve's Weekly', where her fashion illustrations would appear in each issue, making her a known name. When its editor opened a boutique, she asked Bhanu to try designing dresses. She discovered her flair for designing clothes and her success as a designer soon led to her switching career paths. Guru Dutt asked her to design clothes for his films. Starting with C.I.D. in 1956, there was no turning back for her from then on. She worked for five Guru Dutt films. Meanwhile, Bhanu was designing a lot of creations for the boutique. Her customers included actresses Kamini Kaushal and Nargis.

Beginning her career in costume designing over half a century ago, she has created a world of her own that set the standards for costume design in Bollywood cinema. She has done costume designing for 131 films beginning with C.I.D and ending with Swades. She has prepared costumes for six films of Raj Kapoor. Recalling her association with Raj Kapoor, Athaiya writes: "One day Nargis decided to take me to R.K. Studio to introduce me to Raj Kapoor. We travelled to Chembur in her car. As we entered the spacious studio, the first thing I noticed was a huge Shiva statue. Then the car took a left turn and moved towards a small cottage, which was Raj-saab's private cottage. At that time, work on Shri 420 was in progress and I was asked to design costumes for actress Nadira, who was playing a vamp...I gave her an unconventional look."

She has assisted a galaxy of directors, to name a few—Raj Kapoor, Guru Dutt, B.R. Chopra and Ashutosh Gowariker. Among her most memorable output was designing for Waheeda Rehman in Guide, Mumtaz in Brahmachari and Zeenat Aman in Satyam Shivam Sundaram.

Bhanu Athaiya has traced the journey of fashion through films with which she has been associated. She has undoubtedly been a catalyst in defining the contours of Indian fashion. "I knew India and its clothes inside out. I went on a sketching tour as an art student and even spent 10 months in Paris, where I visited all the cabaret joints, including Moulin Rouge," she said. Some of her significant expressions that have indeed become a landmark for Indian films include the looks that she gave to Helen in Teesri Manzil, in the song 'O Haseena Julfon Waali', or the drunk look of Meena Kumari in Sahib Bibi Aur Ghulam. She was able to give Meena Kumari an endearing look even when the canvas of expression had a black and white base.

The book under review is the tale of her tryst with creativity in design. We begin with the utterly fascinating world of black and white world of cinema and graduate to the scintillating world of Technicolour—heavyweights like Sangam, Ganga Jumna and Lagaan. Her pinnacle is of course Gandhi, which fetched the first-ever Oscar for an Indian.

This book is a poem in beauty, which is at once bewitching and highly informative. She unravels the mystery of how she tackled period pieces, which demanded research of extraordinary dimension and total comprehension of Indian mores and traditions. Costume designing gives an actor complete confidence in the role he or she has to play by creating the mood and taking the captive audience to a wholly different and distinct time and clime. What is essential is organisation, artistry, discipline, gifted imagination and patient research—in all of which there is no peer to Athaiya. The costumes she has designed range from the colourful Rajasthani attire set against the desert backdrop, to the typical dress of villagers in the Gangetic plains and the Himalayas. She brought renown for India in the world of international cinema. She got National Awards for two films—Lekin and Lagaan.

One entire chapter is dedicated to the magic of jewellery, which has a hold on Indians and our Gods and Goddesses. Hema Malini in Sanyasi is dressed in resplendent jewellery from head to toe and looks like an *apsara* descended from heavens above. No wonder Manoj Kumar was ensnared! Waheeda Rehman is unforgettable in Reshma and Shera in her colourful *bandhni oddhna* and *ghagra* typical of Rajasthan. Moghul royalty is completely captured by Athaiya in Jodhaa Akbar. The *kilangi jhumki* and other jewellery of this era are brought out in all glory and authenticity. Athaiya has spent hours hunting for period piece jewellery in Hyderabad and other places. "Jewellery is the penultimate touch in the adornment of attire." writes Athaiya.

This is an outstanding book, as evocative as it is colourful and is the complete guide to costume design during the last 50 years in Bollywood. That Athaiya's fame rests not only for Gandhi, but her variegated creations of extraordinary artistry for five long decades becomes abundantly clear as one turns the pages of this luscious book.

23 Journey of a Nation

Shri M.V. Kamath, in one of his recent reviews described the book as 'unputdownable'. The book under review is unarguably one such book. It records the 125 years of the Indian National Congress. Dr Pattabhi Sitaramayya, the pioneer biographer of the Congress wrote perceptively—"Great movements are like great rivers—they start as small streams, but if the cause is great, they draw to themselves many streams, joining together to achieve and reach their destination." The Congress met for the first time with only 72 people in Bombay on 28th December, 1885. It went on to challenge the mightiest empire of the time, using the slogan of peace and the method of non-violence.

This volume is a fascinating record of the struggle for freedom, told in admirably precise fashion, rich in rare photographs and archival material of the highest value. What the reader gets is a bird's-eye view of the tumultuous journey of a nation. Production values are of the highest quality, and Academic Foundation has walked an extra mile to make the journey a pleasure to behold. Special boxes in light colour give photographs and sketches of all Congress Presidents. Important documents and press notices are reproduced.

The book is divided into nine sections. The first section, 'The Formative Years—1885-1920' deals lucidly with the birth of a new party led by men and women of extraordinary courage, commitment culminating

---

Academic Foundation; pp. 306; Price Rs 2995/-.

in India's freedom. Covered are the impact of Dadabhai Naoroji's 'Poverty and Unbritish Rule', the role of Gokhale, Tilak, the split in Surat, the Rowlatt Act and the Jallianwala Bagh massacre.

Section two entitled 'The Gandhian Era' relates to the period 1920-1935. We are privy to Gandhi's struggles, the Simon Commission, the Round Table Conference, and the Dandi March. The section also covers the ascent of Jawaharlal Nehru.

The next section deals with the years 1935-1947. Important events analysed are the Government of India Act, the Congress Ministries, the emergence of Jinnah and the strident demand by the Muslims for creation of Pakistan, Cripps Mission, Quit India Movement, the Cabinet Mission, the Wavell and Mountbatten plans and finally, Independence.

Section four deals with the years 1947-1964. The highlights are the tragic partition, the communal riots, the integration of princely states, the framing of our own Constitution. Nehru inaugurated an era of planning, built a chain of laboratories, and constructed a number of dams, which he called 'The Temples of Modern India'. He made 'Non-alignment' an acceptable philosophy.

The next section analyses the Congress party's role from 1964 to 1994. Nehru was succeeded by Lal Bahadur Shastri. India was embroiled in a war with Pakistan. Shastri died and was followed by Indira Gandhi, who was Prime Minister for 15 years—in two terms. She nationalised 14 major banks, abolished privy purses. The 1971 war with Pakistan transformed her into 'Durga' and led to creation of Bangladesh. The Shimla Agreement and the Pokhran nuclear tests followed. She declared Emergency after a court order disqualified her, leading on to her defeat in the 1977 elections. The Janata government and the 1980 elections swept her back to power. 'The Operation Bluestar' led to her assassination.

The remaining sections dwell on the Rajiv Gandhi era. He introduced computerisation, brought peace to Punjab, Assam and Mizoram. The Bofors deal and internal party dissensions led to fresh general elections. Rajiv Gandhi was assassinated by the LTTE agents. The book recalls the advent of P.V. Narasimha Rao and economic reforms initiated by Manmohan Singh. The destruction of Babri Masjid caused turmoil in the country. Sonia Gandhi became Congress President. The Bharatiya Janata Party (BJP) led National Democratic Alliance (NDA) was in power from 1998-2004. The Godhra massacre followed by riots are dealt with. The coalition government led by Manmohan Singh followed. The last section lays down the agenda for the future, which is 'inclusive growth'. 'This volume is both a remembrance of things past and a commemoration of the long journey the Indian National Congress has travelled.'

This is a volume to cherish and read by all students, politicians of every hue and disciples of history. The book is truly an achievement and accomplishment.

24 History in the Making: The Visual Archives of Kulwant Roy

This is a magnificent coffee-table book containing a priceless collection of photographs by Kulwant Roy from the 1930s to 1960s. The prints and negatives of these photographs remained forgotten in boxes for over 25 years after his death in 1984. The world must be thankful to their inheritor Aditya Arya, a photographer himself, for making it available. Arya, while cataloguing them, stumbled upon a rare and valuable visual archive, including many unpublished pictures, of a momentous era in India's history. Some of these unusual pictures relate to Muslim League meetings, Indian National Army (INA) trials, the signing of the Indian Constitution, as well as significant post-Independence milestones such as the building of the Bhakra Nangal Dam. Indivar Kamtekar, an eminent historian, provides an illuminating text. All those who wish to pierce the veil behind India's 'tryst with destiny' must dip into this classic volume.

Author Aditya Arya graduated in history from St Stephen's College, Delhi and plunged into professional photography. He has acquired expertise in the world of advertising and corporate photography. His works have been exhibited the world over, and his photographs have been published by renowned global journals. He is the author of

---

Harper Collins; pp. 336; Price Rs 4999/-.

'The Land of the Nagas', a photographic documentation of the Naga people and the first ever exhaustive visual study of the masterpieces of Buddhist art at the Alchi monastery in Ladakh. Indivar Kamtekar is a name to reckon with in the field of teaching. He teaches modern history at the Jawaharlal Nehru University and has been a faculty member of the Indian Institute of Management, Calcutta, and a fellow of the Indian Institute of Advanced Study, Shimla. For his doctoral thesis from Cambridge, he selected the end of British rule in India.

Kulwant Roy was an Indian photographer, who was born in Lahore in 1914. As the head of the 'Associated Press Photographs' he secured several iconic images of the Indian independence movement and the early years of the Republic of India. He joined the Royal Indian Air Force (RIAF) and specialised in aerial photography. After relinquishing his link with the RIAF, he moved to Delhi in 1940 and set up a studio, which later expanded into a full-fledged agency, in the Mori Gate district of Old Delhi. This area was to become an important centre of Press photographs in the country. He followed Mahatma Gandhi, for a number of years in his travels around India in a third-class train compartment; this endowed him with an insider status that meant that he was permitted to record many crucial events of and major participants in the independence movement, including Jinnah, Nehru and Patel—surely the dream of any photographer. Roy covered Jacqueline Kennedy's visit in 1962 to India and India's war with Pakistan in 1965.

To Kulwant Roy's utter dismay, he noted that a new breed of aggressive young photojournalists acquired dominance. He heartily disliked this and hung up his camera and faded into obscurity. "No one knew him or his past," Arya said. Roy was a frequent visitor to Arya's parents' home in New Delhi, having known Arya's mother's family from Lahore. But by the time Arya was old enough to remember him, Roy was a poor and lonely man. "He never wanted me to be a photographer because of the hardships and the fact that one has to live a life a bit like a vagabond," said Arya. Roy died of cancer, virtually penniless and with no children of his own and left Arya his photo collection.

Arya is now dedicated to restoring Roy to what he sees as his proper place in the annals of Indian photojournalism. Roy sold many of his photographs to international news agencies during his lifetime and some of them are now found in archival collections, but they are rarely credited with his name. "For me making sure people know his name is as important as making sure they know his pictures," declared Arya. Arya believes that some of the images—for instance, a picture of a loin-clothed Gandhi descending from a third-class rail car—could become as iconic as the vintage India photos taken by the celebrated Margaret Bourke-White and Cartier-Bresson. Again, Nehru's hand curled tenderly around grandson Rajiv's neck, Gandhi and Jinnah arguing in 1939, Nehru and Ghaffar Khan strolling in Shimla—these nuggets of history were captured through photographs by Kulwant Roy from 1940 to 1960.

Roy thoughtfully selected frames that attempt to capture moments of time that will make one pause, and revive hidden memory. This is an ultimate treasure trove for anyone, who loves photography. There are a wide range of rare exhibits from Roy's collection. He captured various moods, showing glimpses of political leaders in different facets of life. He, with his photographs, threw light on last years of British rule, but didn't get the recognition. Moreover, he captured off-the-cuff moments of great leaders making them approachable figures. Roy's photos depict rare glimpses of pre and post-Independence era and freedom fighters, who have endured many years of conflict. We have rare photographs of the visit of Gandhi to meet Khan Abdul Ghaffar Khan in the North East frontier province, visit of Sir Stafford Cripps to India in 1941, Simla Conference in 1945, Muslim League meetings, fund raising by Gandhi, building of Bhakra dam, and visits of dignitaries.

The nationalist movement is covered by tracing mainstream politics through portraits. Wonderful images of Mahatma Gandhi collecting money from a woman for Harijan fund, Mahatma Gandhi addressing members of INA at Harijan colony, Delhi have been captured by Roy.

It is a mystery when a news photographer, makes history from deadline to deadline, never really knowing when he might take a photograph that will determine how an entire era is remembered. Consider the famous photograph of Jawaharlal Nehru, Mahatma Gandhi and Sardar Vallabhbhai Patel at a Congress meeting in 1946. Gandhi, looking into the middle distance, is, as ever, talking mainly to himself; Nehru and Patel, one on either side, straining to listen in; Nehru looking intently at his mentor's mouth; and Patel's face showing the effort it took for him to lean over at an uncomfortable, 45 degree angle. Could Roy have dreamt when he took it that it would be the most memorable representation of those strained relationships? It was chosen as the basis for a commemorative stamp after Patel died.

Turning the pages of this majestic volume holds a lesson for us, which is that, great men influenced history, but they did not control it. Manmohan Singh in his foreword has rightly written "...History in the making takes us back in time to a momentous and inspirational chapter of our past. The images captured by photojournalist Kulwant Roy bring alive the years which saw the birth of an independent India. Kulwant Roy's photographs are sources as well as products of India. I hope that more such visual archives are brought to light and given the recognition and importance they richly deserve."

One tragic note. Roy travelled to Japan, Hong Kong, USA, Panama, Brazil and various European countries. The negatives and prints of photographs taken there were mailed back to his address in Delhi, but were never delivered. A shattered man, he spent the next few years looking for the negatives and prints in garbage dumps and open spaces around Delhi.

We welcome such breathtaking books as also the India Photo Archive Foundation, which has been established to identify, preserve and document photographic legacies like the output of Kulwant Roy. It will contribute towards creating a culture of dialogue on diverse narratives of photographic archives, which are landmarks of history.

Travels

TRAVELS »

25 Travels in the Americas

US Cops Baffled by Lakshmy

The scene is the 'Logan Airport' in Boston, the date June 29th, the hour 7 am. The three of us had motored down for over an hour through densely crowded traffic from Chelmsford to the airport. We planned to take the American Airlines flight to San Francisco at 9 am. We checked in and handed over our baggage and proceeded to the security check. They asked us to place on separate boxes, all the contents of our attire—purse, loose coins, watches, ball pens, belt and even the sweater we wore. Also, the footwear was to be taken off and subjected to a strict check.

While Pushpa and I sailed through smoothly, there was something with Lakshmy that attracted the pointed attention of the security staff. Two burly, hefty policewomen duly attired in deep black holsters with guns on either side (so that they can shoot left and right) proceeded to move the detector over her body. The moment they crossed over her waist, they were startled by a peculiar noise. Lakshmy was wearing a black nylon saree with a floral design. "But what is this noise?" they asked themselves. Perhaps this tiny lady has concealed a dangerous weapon! What is it? They pondered over. They moved the scanner up and down. One cop told the other, "This sure is a mystery wrapped in a riddle concealed in an enigma," quoting Winston Churchill, whose mother Sarah was born in USA. Lakshmy innocently declared, "It is a safety pin without which my saree will not remain in place!" and she showed them the innocent safety pin.

Scarcely happy in their failure to detect any offensive weapon of mass destruction (WMD), they proceeded to examine her with scrupulous American precision. "Lady, please put your left foot forward." And Lakshmy of India was enjoying it very much. The policewomen barked, "Now put your right foot behind." She did this with more joy. The scanner went up like a yo-yo up and down! Alas! Of no avail were the efforts of these successors of Pinkerton! "Kindly remove your bangles." This was complied with some difficulty as Lakshmy has put on weight drinking hot chocolates and demolishing croissants! At last she showed them the bangles made in Chembur. The *hidimbis* scanned it with a wry smile. No luck for them with this Indian lady. "O.K. you are clean. You can go!" Lakshmy was thrilled that she could offer so much entertainment and challenge to the US police. We were eager to have a photo clicked of Lakshmy with a raised arm smiling at an American cop, but photography is banned in this sector.

We proceeded to the lounge and were waiting for an announcement to board the aircraft. At 8.45 they announced cancellation of the flight! Poor Pushpa had to go through the Himalayan task of getting alternative tickets. She did it. This had one gain. We flew via Chicago instead of Dallas, which we had touched en route. But we had to go through the dreadful process of retrieving our luggage and checking in once more and going through security check again. The same whipper-snapper cops but they smiled at Lakshmy and said, "Ma'am, you are one clean one!" And thus, we boarded the aircraft.

If you recall, it was from this 'Logan Airport' that the two agents of Al Qaeda took off to destroy the World Trade Centre! Security has become a disease with the Americans.

Niagara Falls

Our journey to the great Niagara Falls began with a drive of 220 miles from Pittsburg by car, driven by Pushpa. She was driving for the first time to Niagara and she took the assistance of the global positioning system (GPS). We reached by 7 pm and checked in at the Travelodge, which she had already booked for two days. We were on the 9th floor, and you have to use two plastic cards to open your room. Keys are no more used in hotels! Scrupulously clean with a fridge and TV. We were exhausted by the drive and decided to take a *dekko* in the morning. Meanwhile, we could hear the torrent from this distance. We had an electric cooker with us and Lakshmy made *upma*. It came out exquisitely well. The thought of making South Indian *upma* in a hotel in Niagara regaled me no end. She did it in New York too. We slept and after breakfast, we walked down for 10 minutes to the Falls.

There are a number of ways to enjoy the ferocious beauty of the thundering cataracts. Popular is the 'Maid of the Mist', which takes you by boat for half an hour to the foot of the American and Canadian waterfalls. They provide you with raincoats and special shoes, which you can retain. The moment the boat starts moving water splashes on your face and within moments I was sightless, my specs becoming totally wet. The boat moves at great speed and one has to cling to the railings. In our helpless state, Pushpa snapped a few pictures on her digital camera.

'The Bridal Veil' is the name given to the pure white stretch of water from which we can see rainbows. A second option is the 'Cave of the Winds Tour'. Truly out of this world! You take an elevator ride down 175 feet to the base of the 'Bridal Veil'. Along the base, they have constructed wooden steps on the rocks, which we ascend to touch just 35 feet below the 'Bridal Veil'. This calls for some courage and determination. Both Lakshmy and I went up to the top. You experience the power of the Niagara Falls from the 'Hurricane Deck' just a few feet from the crashing descent! Standing at the brink, your pulse quickens at this magnificent sight. You can feel the earth shake at your feet as the water rushes over the brink casting its spell on you.

A third and simple way is to walk along the park and see the glory of God's creation. When I was a pimply school boy, I had seen at Aurora—the Hollywood flick, Niagara starring Joseph Cotten, Robert Mitchum and the incomparable Miss Marilyn Monroe. Though there were impressive pictures of the waterfall, I was more impressed by the curves of Miss Monroe, and for long considered that superior to the cataract! That foolish vision vanished now, only after seeing the real Niagara. Magnificent in beauty, serene in its descent and a sight never to be forgotten!

The Niagara Falls are on the international line between the cities of Niagara Falls in USA and Niagara Falls in Ontario. The Goat Island splits the cataract into the 'American Falls' —184 feet high and 1,050 feet wide—on the American side and the 'Horseshoe Falls' —176 feet high and 2,219 feet wide on the Canadian side.

The earliest description of the falls is that of Levis Hennep in 1697. He was with the expedition of Robert Cavalier, a French explorer. The Niagara River is 34 miles long, issuing from Lake Erie between Buffalo, New York, USA and Fort Erie, Ontario, Canada. Every evening the falls are illuminated with changing colours by 24 gigantic search lights. Excellent views of the Falls may be had from such sites as 'Prospect Point', 'Table Rock' and 'Terrapin Point'. The falls are the 49th highest falls in the world and the third greatest in the power and volume of water that flows over them. Total flow is 212,000 cubic feet per second. The falls gets its name from the Neutre Indians and means 'Thundering Waters'. On the American side there is a pool called 'Maid of the Mist' and extends for about 2.5 miles down the gorge from the base of the falls and is navigated by two boats called 'Maid of the Mist'.

Both Canada and USA have exploited the Niagara river for hydroelectric power.

The falls have been the scene of many daredevil exploits ever since Sam Patch in 1829 successfully leaped into the river twice, only to lose his life in Rochester in a similar leap at the Genesee Falls. Several men and women have safely plunged over one or the other fall or through the whirlpool in barrels. And in 1860, Blondin performed amazing feats on a tightrope stretched across the gorge.

It is interesting to read of the exploits of a 43 year old widowed teacher, Mrs Anna Edson Taylor, who on October 24, 1901 squeezed herself into a specially constructed barrel measuring four and a half feet high and three feet in diameter. For protection she had leather shoulder straps and cushions. At her feet was a 700 lb blacksmith's anvil to keep the craft upright in the water. Her air supply came from a rubber hose connected to a small opening near the lid.

A boat towed the barrel and passenger to a point near Grass Island. At 4.05 the line was cut and the barrel shot down the stream, bobbing crazily. At 4.23 it reached the brink of the Horseshoe Falls on the Canadian side, paused there for a moment and plummeted 176 feet straight down into the swirling eddies below. For 60 long seconds the barrel disappeared from sight before it finally popped up several 100 yards below the falls. Seventeen minutes later a team of men recovered the barrel, which had to be sawed apart to extricate the dizzy female daredevil. She had been knocked unconscious and blood was flowing from a three inch gash on her forehead. When she recovered enough so to speak, Mrs Taylor warned others- "Never to attempt the foolish thing I have done."

Golden Gate

We drove to San Francisco starting at 8.30 am. It was a 45 minute drive. There was a lot of mist and it was quite chilly. The first view of the Golden Gate was that of a huge structure cocooned in clouds and only 10 per cent visible. After parking our vehicle we began walking towards the bridge. The bridge has been the basis for three works of fiction—Alistair MacLean's 'Golden Gate', followed by Colin Forbes's 'Year of the Golden Ape' and Vikram Seth's 'The Golden Gate', a novel in poetic form mainly quatrains.

I had also total recall of the Hitchcock movie Vertigo, where dark doe-eyed Kim Novak attempts to kill herself at the southern end of the bridge and her being rescued by James Stewart. At last, I was seeing the bridge that has become a symbol of San Francisco as also America. And in sunlight, what a bridge and what an engineering marvel! The sample of the suspension cable is so thick that it reminds you of the leg of an elephant and it is packed with wire rope of great strength. The bridge is somewhat curved and once it was supposed to have bent further with over a million people walking on it. Thereafter, they banned such a collection of people on the bridge. We walked along the bridge and the mist lifted, and we could clearly see the sea as also the stark Alcatraz, the world's highest security prison. For me it meant two movies—The Birdman of Alcatraz with Burt Lancaster and The Rock with Sean Connery. I shall write of Alcatraz later. Meanwhile, we walked on the bridge freezing in the cold air. Lots of tourists—several in scanty attire! How they could bear the cold, we wondered. Half way about a mile—we returned and did the rest of the tour by car. Pushpa drove us on the bridge and Anand drove on the way back. The small peak on Marin County afforded us a different view of the bridge, which was quite breathtaking with San Francisco houses in a lovely cluster.

Those with interest in the Golden Gate read on.

The Golden Gate was declared open in May 1937 after four years of construction. It links San Francisco with Marin County. The bridge is 2 miles long with a main span of 4,200 feet. It was the longest suspension bridge when it was constructed. The 746 feet suspension towers were higher than any New York structure. Joseph B. Strauss, the bridge's builder was a specialist in steel bridge design, who had built more than 400 bridges all over the world. The bridge's name comes from the nickname given to the entrance to the harbour by early visitors. Its actual colour is international orange. Painting the bridge is a never-ending job. A team of 25 painters adds another thousand gallons every week.

The Fort Point lookout from where you can start has a statue of Strauss and a sample of the 3 feet thick suspension cable. The north end is the Vista Point. The view from here has San Francisco as the backdrop. There are three lanes with separate access for walkers, cyclists and cars and other vehicles.

Eleven men died during construction of the bridge and it has continued to be the favourite suicide spot. It is a 200 feet drop from the bridge to the water. If the impact doesn't kill one immediately, the swift current will take him to the sea with the likelihood of being drowned or eaten by sharks. Despite these factors, some have survived the bridge jumps, including an 18 year old woman who jumped twice in 1988. She survived the first jump, but not the second. In 1995, there occurred the 1000th leap to death. There was a rush to be the 1000th entrant into the Hall of Fame or infamy! USA is notorious for such feats! A suicide barrier was proposed, but voted out as it would spoil the aesthetic beauty of the bridge. Ironically, proposals for the suicide barrier once included the one by the Rev Jim Jones, whose moving anti-suicide speech in 1977 was undermined a year later when Jones himself led a mass suicide of over 200 persons in Guyana.

The Empire State Building

Hollywood has cast its magic spell on me from the age of five and for almost 64 years, I have been a willing victim to its charms. One of the movies that captured my childish imagination was King Kong (1933) in which a monster sought refuge in the tower of the Empire State Building. Another classic movie was An Affair to Remember with Cary Grant and Deborah Kerr in which the star crossed lovers are scheduled to meet in the 86th floor of this building, and the vivacious Miss Kerr is injured by a speeding car and is not able to make it to the top. It was this tower that Laskhmy and I, led by Pushpa, ascended on a misty morn.

It is the most famous landmark of New York City. It was the tallest building in the world at the time of its completion in 1931 and remained so till 1970. The unprecedented height of the building led to many interesting comparisons. For example, if the Eiffel tower were piled over the great pyramid of Cheops, the Empire State Building would still exceed their combined height by 38 feet. Pennies tossed off the building's observation deck will never reach the street below, much less cause danger to any pedestrians. The building's spire acts as a lightning rod to the entire city. It gets struck in excess of 100 times per year. Some 3.8 million people visit the tower's observation deck annually, making it the most frequently visited and most recognisable skyscraper in the world. A bomber crashed into the 79th floor of the building in 1945. Damage was confined to the outer wall, preserving the tower's structural integrity.

The 102 storey building measures 1,250 feet from the sidewalk to the roof. The architectural firm of Shrove, Lamb and Harman designed the tower, which is an epitome of building skill. It rises in a series of step like shapes called setbacks to a slender tower topped by a metal spire. Panels of limestone and an alloy of chrome, nickel and steel cover the skyscraper's riveted steel structure.

The Empire State Building has some impressive statistics. Every year there is a race to see who can get to the top by climbing its 1,860 steps. The building has 6,500 windows. Seventy-three elevators operate at speeds ranging from 600 to 1,200 feet per minute and occupy 7 miles of shaft. The building contains 2,284,000 square feet of rentable space. The building is powered by 2,500,000 feet of electrical wire. The sinks and toilets connect to 70 miles of pipes.

The tower has captured the attention of old and young alike, and every year millions of tourists flock to the 86th and 102nd floor observatories and get a heavenly glimpse of New York City.

The Statue of Liberty

There are several ways to travel in this vast American continent. One is to fly, which is costly. Another is to drive, which is tiresome. A third is to tour by the 'Greyhound' a reputed bus service, which will transport you from Seattle to Orlando, to any place in USA and at considerably cheap rates and admirable convenience. We took this mode to travel from Washington to New York.

As we neared New York we could see the famous Manhattan skyline with skyscrapers like the Empire State Building, the Chrysler building, the Rockefeller Centre and many others. In the distance we could see the Statue of Liberty as well. This was our next target. After settling down in a hotel in Central Park, we took 'the hop on and hop off' bus and went to the entrance to the Statue of Liberty. After standing in a queue for over an hour, we entered the boat that took us to the island, which housed the monument.

We found an impressive well attired American claiming that he was Bartholdi, who made the statue, and he carried a rolled chart of the plan of the monument. He tried to impress us, but was distinctly disappointed by my remark that I want to remind him of the famous statement of Mark Twain. That was, "We erect statues to those that are dead and the greatest of them all is the Statue of Liberty!" Mark Twain not withstanding, the monument is one of the most impressive things I have seen, though its green colour was off putting. For those interested in this lady, read on.

A gigantic statue on Liberty Island (formerly Bedloe's Island) in New York harbour, the statue was originally called 'Liberty enlightening the world'. It was placed to face the harbour as a symbol to arriving voyagers of the freedom and opportunity that was offered by USA. The statue represents a regal woman draped in classical robes and wearing a crown with seven spokes, each standing for the light of liberty shining on the seven seas and the seven continents. At her feet lie the broken shackles of slavery. In the uplifted right hand she carries a torch, and in her left hand she holds a law book in which are inscribed the words 'July 4, 1776', the date of the declaration of Independence.

The figure is made of large hammered copper plates welded to a steel alloy. Exposure to weather gives the figure a rich green colour. It weighs 225 tonnes and is 155 feet and 1 inch high to the top of the torch. The pedestal is 89 feet high and the base is 69 feet above the level of the bay, making the elevation 313 feet and 1 inch above sea level.

An elevator takes visitors to the top of the statue's pedestal. From there two spiral staircases climb through the hollow statue into the figure's crown, where windows provide a spectacular view of the harbour. At night, the statue, including the crown and torch, is illuminated by floodlights and special lamps.

The statue was a gift, made in 1884, from the people of France to the

US in commemoration of the centennial of American Independence. The statue was designed by Frederic Bartholdi; the iron framework was designed by Gustave Eiffel, who later created the Eiffel tower in Paris. Money for the monument was raised by subscription from the French people. The figure was built in Paris, disassembled and shipped to New York, where a pedestal had been raised for the statue with funds raised from Americans.

The total cost of monument was $800,000. France donated $400,000. It was dedicated by the American President Cleveland in October, 1886.

In 1903, Emma Lazarus's sonnet to the statue 'The New Colossus' was inscribed in a bronze plaque in the pedestal.

Not like the brazen giant of Greek fame,
With conquering limbs astride from land to land
her at our sea-washed sunset gates shall stand
A mighty woman with a torch, whose flame
is the imprisoned lightning, and her name
Mother of exiles. From her beacon hand
the air-bridged harbour that twin cities frame
"Keep ancient lands your storied pomp!"–she cries
with silent lips. "Give me your tired poor
Your huddled masses yearning to breathe fame,
send these the homeless tempest tost to me,
I lift my lamp beside the golden door."

The idea for the statue came from Edouard Labolaye, a French politician who admired the US. He proposed construction of a joint French and American monument celebrating the idea of liberty. Bartholdi modelled the statue after the face of his mother.

Pittsburg

Pittsburg is the second largest city in Pennsylvania state.

It lies in the rolling hills of southwest Pennsylvania, where the

Allegheny and the Monongahela rivers meet and form the Ohio river. During late 1880s, Pittsburg was the world's largest producer of steel. Because of the smoke from the steel mills it was called 'Smoky City'. But the name that stuck is 'The Steel City'. It was named after William Pitt, later the Prime Minister of England. Pittsburg has over 450 bridges—more than any other city in USA. A hill called Mt Washington overlooks the city and is 450 feet high and stretches several miles across the Monongahela River. It has several observation decks that offer spectacular views of Pittsburg and its three rivers. Two small cable car lines called 'Inclines' carry visitors up and down the mount. We travelled by the one called the 'Duquesne Incline'.

Pittsburg is the centre of the world famous Carnegie Mellon University, which houses the Carnegie library, one of the largest in USA. It is named after Andrew Carnegie, an industrialist turned benefactor. There is a Carnegie science museum, which is very impressive and has the largest skeleton of a dinosaur.

The University of Pittsburg main college building is a 42 storey building and has the cathedral of learning. Entering this cathedral is like entering the holiest of holy temples. The nationality rooms here are a tribute to the heritages of the city's ethnic groups. Funded by these communities, they are designed by renowned architects from abroad. The rooms adapt Classical, Byzantine, Baroque, Renaissance, Tudor, Empire and Folk styles to recreate cultural periods prior to 1787, the founding date of the University.

A visit to the nationality rooms is virtually a mini tour of 26 heritages in a time warp, which transports us from 5th century Greece, through 1st century Israel, and 7th century India to Poland of 16th century. Original and recreated furnishings combine with carved stone, stained glass, sculptured and inlaid wood to provide unforgettable glimpses of European, Middle Eastern, African and Asian cultures.

Of course we were keen on India. The style of architecture is monastic 4th-9th century. As soon as you enter the room, the loud chanting of the 'Sikshavali' from the 'Taittiriya Upanishad' greets you—*mathru devo bhava, pithru devo bhava, acharya devo bhava, athithi devo bhava*—rendered quite pleasingly. They have used Nalanda University as the motif. One finds statues of Buddha, Mahavira, several Hindu Gods and Goddesses. I searched for the Asoka pillar. Thought it was missing and a major omission. Eggregiously wrong PPR. They had placed it just above the entrance. Rich references to our hoary past and cultural achievements made me proud to be an Indian.

The nationality room of England, of course, had items dear to my heart and head—William Shakespeare, Milton, and Dickens. The Germans had their brothers Grimm and Denmark, of course, Hans Christian Anderson. In all, 26 countries are represented. All halls are closed. You are given a key with which you open when you enter and have to close when you have seen each room. They give you a tape recorder and this has a commentary for each country. Splendid work indeed. Makes the trip to Pittsburg truly memorable!

Facing the Cathedral is the Heinz memorial chapel, declared open in 1938. It was a gift from Henry John Heinz, founder of Heinz Company Recall Heinz sauce. (Actually their main factory is in Pittsburgh and they have a giant sauce bottle in front of the factory). Coming back to the chapel, it is dedicated to culture, an understanding response to beauty and religious worship. Various religious services are held in the chapel, but it belongs to no single denomination. Many simply seek its peace and beauty as a refuge. It has got some of the most splendidly etched stained glass. The lower half has etchings of biblical characters, Old Testament prophets, patriarchs, priests, King David. The upper half is a glimpse of the world's great men and women. I could find out Leonardo Da Vinci, Isaac Newton, Louis Pasteur, William Wordsworth, Albert Einstein, Charles Dickens, Abraham Lincoln, Florence Nightingale, Madame Curie and Mark Twain. A noteworthy aspect is that men and women are represented equally.

After dealing with such cerebral items it is refreshing to visit the national aviary, where you are in a giant glass house in which a forest has been created. Birds of all types and hues abound here in natural environment. Happily we went at feeding time. They ask us to hold fruits and worms in our hands, and the birds pluck it from your hand so speedily that we cannot capture photos even with our digital camera. They were very colourful and very entertaining. The sounds, shapes and colours of birds were myriad. From here we went to the Phipps Conservatory and botanical gardens. Designed by Lord and Burnham and donated by Henry Phipps, the conservatory has delighted millions of flower and plant enthusiasts from the world over.

Indians can scarcely skip the Sri Venkateswara temple of Pittsburg. It is a mini Tirupati and fabulously rich. It is the oldest Hindu temple in USA and has attracted lot of worshippers. More impressive than the temple was the attractive, delectable, very tasty *thair satham*, *puliyodharai* and *rava kesari*. All these are given free, immediately after *pooja*. At other times it is available for a nominal payment. One solid reason to visit Pittsburg I discovered, was this feature. I noticed that in Mumbai they give white *til gul*, whereas here they give *badams*, oranges and apples. I found, sometimes, they distributed full *laddoos*! The benefits to be gained from temple visits are indeed sizable, memorable and delectable.

Boston-Harvard-MIT

Boston is a place to be reckoned with in American history, as it was from here that the spark was lit that led to the American revolt against the British rulers. Known as 'The Boston Tea Party', the incident occurred on 16th December, 1773, in which American patriots dumped into the Boston Bay, tea belonging to the English East India Company—the same Company that ruled us too. Sixty Americans dressed as 'Mohawk Indians' boarded three ships and threw out into the bay, chests of tea valued at 18,000 pounds. England took firm steps and this emboldened the American resistance and led to throwing out of the British.

Boston today is unique for its centres of learning, the Harvard University, the Massachusetts Institute of Technology (MIT) and the Boston University.

Harvard is the oldest institution of higher learning in USA and was founded in Cambridge, Massachusetts in 1636, barely 15 years after the 'Pilgrim Fathers' landed in Plymouth. A young minister, John Harvard, dying of tuberculosis, bequeathed in 1638—his library of 400 volumes and half his estate to the infant college newly started by 100 graduates from Oxford and Cambridge universities of UK. The bequest amounted to 779 pounds, which was a princely sum then.

At its inception, Harvard was under church sponsorship, but during its first two centuries the College liberated itself, first from clerical and later political control, until in 1865 the University alumni began elections to the Governing Board. During his 40 year tenure as President, Mr C.W. Eliot made Harvard into an institution with national influence. Harvard produced 40 Nobel laureates. Some of the great students of Harvard are Emerson, Thoreau, T.S. Eliot and Walter Lippmann. Seven American presidents, who graduated from Harvard are John Adams, John Quincy Adams, Theodore Roosevelt, Franklin Roosevelt, Rutherford Hayes, J.F. Kennedy and George Bush. India's Subramaniam Swamy and Amartya Sen lectured here for some years, the former on Chinese and the latter on Economics.

Harvard has 17 separate departments, 95 libraries, 7 botanical institutions, 2 astronomical stations, 50 laboratories of science, engineering, medicine and 9 museums of natural history. There are divinity schools and a law school. The Central University Library has over 12 million books. The endowment today is above four billion dollars.

An impressive statue of John Harvard is a star attraction. Cast in 1884, it is known as 'The Statue of Three Lies'. Although the inscription reads 'John Harvard, Founder, 1638,' none of these three statements is true. The seated figure could be anybody, since no authentic pictures of Mr Harvard existed; John Harvard was not the founder (he was the first benefactor); and the College was founded in 1636. Tourists rub Harvard's shoes for good luck.

There is a Harvard Square at the entrance facing, which is the Harvard Coop—a bookstall that has three floors. You can pick up any book and settle down in a comfy sofa and read for as long as you like. Excellent cafeteria facilities obtain. I saw the table from where J.K. Galbraith wrote portions of his book 'The Affluent Society'. The only thing I could do was to buy a doughnut and eat it and quaff hot chocolate!

After visiting Harvard it is time to visit MIT. The MIT is a private institution of higher learning. Founded in 1861, MIT has become famous for its scientific research activities and for combining education and research in all programmes. It has special departments in Aeronautics, Astronautics, Architecture, Physics and Chemistry, Chemical Technology, Foreign Literature and Metallurgy. MIT has its own Nuclear Reactor, Centre for Cancer Research, and Centre for Space Research.

The Boston University established in 1869 is also a private non-sectarian university and has 16 schools and colleges. Of the three institutions, it is the youngest but fast acquiring fame and name.

Washington DC

Washington is situated in the north-east bank of the Potomac river. The Washington skyline is dominated by the Capitol because of its size, central location and elevated position on Capitol Hill. The US Congress meets in this building. It is constructed of white sandstone and marble and is crowned by an immense dome. On top of the dome stands a bronze 19.5 feet Statue of Freedom. Public rooms include a rotunda decorated with paintings and statues of events and people in American history.

To the east is the Supreme Court modelled after a Greek temple. Nearby stands the Library of Congress, one of the largest in the world, the Lenin library in Moscow being larger.

Washington Monument

The Washington Monument, the world's tallest free standing work of masonry is a white marble column about 555 feet high. Its interior is hollow. Climbing the 897 steps is not allowed, but large elevators whisk visitors in just 70 seconds to the top for a panoramic view. Like the centre of a compass, it provides a marvellous orientation to the city. 193 carved stones are inserted into the interior walls. The stones are gifts from foreign countries, all 50 states, organisations and individuals. The most expensive stone was given by Alaska in 1982—it is pure jade and worth millions of dollars.

Lincoln Memorial

The Lincoln Memorial situated in the west Potomac Park was designed by Henry Bacon. The neo-classical temple-like structure is similar to the Parthenon in Greece. Its exterior is a white marble colonnade, consisting of 36 Doric columns representing the 36 states of the Union at the time of Lincoln's death. Due east is the reflecting pool, lined with American elms and stretching 2,000 feet towards the Washington monument.

Inside is the 19 feet statue of Abraham Lincoln in contemplation designed by Daniel Chester French. In the sidewalls, carved on massive stone tablets are texts of the Gettysburg address and Lincoln's second inaugural address.

You derive an impression of solemn dignity and nobility associated with the memory of Lincoln. Lincoln's legacy has made this memorial the site of numerous demonstrations by those seeking justice. Most notable was a peaceful demonstration, on August 28, 1963, led by Martin Luther King at which he delivered his famous proclamation "I Have A Dream." It is one of the most eloquent expressions of African-American aspirations. Over 2,50,000 Americans heard him spellbound.

Jefferson Memorial

President Kennedy at a 1962 dinner honouring 29 Nobel Prize winners told his guests that they were "the most extraordinary collection of talent, of human knowledge that has ever been gathered together at the White House, with the possible exception when Thomas Jefferson dined alone." Jefferson, who penned the Declaration of Independence was George Washington's Secretary of State and John Adam's Vice-President and the third American President. He established the Virginia University, and his interests included architecture, astronomy anthropology, music and farming. F.D. Roosevelt had all the trees between the memorial and the White House cut down so that he could see the memorial every morning. The domed interior of the memorial contains the 19 feet bronze statue of Jefferson standing on a 6 feet pedestal of black granite. Jefferson is depicted wearing a fur coat that was gifted to him by his close friend, a Polish General.

Library of Congress

The books of the Library of Congress are on the 532 miles of shelves located throughout the Library's three buildings—the Thomas Jefferson, James Madison Memorial and the John Adams building. Established in 1800 'for the purchase of such books as may be necessary for the use of Congress', the library serves the nation today. Its first collection of books was destroyed in 1814 when the British burnt the Capitol where the library was then located, during the war of 1812. Thomas Jefferson sold the institution his personal library of 6,847 books as a replacement, and this became the foundation of the second largest library in the world.

The collection contains a mind-boggling 128 million items. There are 29 million catalogued books, 57 million manuscripts, 12 million prints and photographs, 2.7 million audio holdings, a million movies and videotapes, musical instruments from the 1700s and the letters and papers of everyone from George Washington to Groucho Marx. The architecture is magnificent. Fifty painters and sculptors worked for eight years on the interior of the Jefferson building. There are floor mosaics of Italian marble, allegorical paintings on the overhead vaults, more than 100 murals, and numerous ornamental cornucopias, ribbons, vines and garlands. The main reading room has a 160 feet dome. The American treasures of the Library of Congress has rare items—such as the rough draft of Jefferson's Declaration of

Independence with notes by Benjamin Franklin and John Adams in the margin. Here are the contents of Lincoln's pockets when he was assassinated.

On the walls are famous quotations without naming the writers. It is believed that one must go to the library and find out the authors. We heard and saw the film in which Groucho Marx was interviewed by Johnny Carson, and where the former gifted his entire works to the library. It was at once humorous as only Groucho can be, and touching as well.

Ford's Theatre

We visited the Ford's theatre, where the first American Presidential assassination was enacted. John Wilkes Booth, an actor in Shakespearean plays was the man who struck down Abraham Lincoln. On April 14, 1865, the President and his wife were seated in a box with Major Henry Rathbone and his fiancee Clara Harris. General Ulysses Grant and his wife were invited, but begged off the last moment. The play they were watching was Tom Taylor's comedy, 'Our American Cousin'.

Here is how it happened. Booth, well known in the theatre enters the Presidential box and bars the door behind him. About 10.15 pm, he points a derringer at the back of Lincoln's head and fires once. Rathbone tries to grab Booth, but Booth slashes him severely with a hunting knife. Booth, then leaps to the stage, but his spur catches the draped flag. He breaks his leg in the fall. Fleeing Booth shouts *Sic Temper Tyrannis* (thus always to tyrants)—the motto of Virginia state. Booth escapes on a horse he had kept in an alley. Doctors carried President Lincoln across the street. He never regained consciousness and died the next morning at 7.22 am. Secretary of war, Edwin Stanton announced, "Now he belongs to the ages." The derringer pistol used by Booth as also his diary outlining his rationalisation for the deed is in the Lincoln Museum.

Mount Vernon Estate

You can soak yourself in the life and times of George Washington in his estate and gardens at Mount Vernon. The centrepiece of a visit to this 500 acre estate is the tour through 14 rooms of the mansion dating from 1740s. Washington inherited this from his great-grandfather in 1754, and in the next 45 years developed it to his liking. You can see original furnishings used by the Washington family. You can tour through the kitchens, slave quarters, storeroom, etc. In the farms, 18th century farming methods are on display. There is a wharf and you can go in a boat on the Potomac River. A tomb contains the remains of the President, his wife and 24 other members of his family.

Mount Vernon is owned by the Mount Vernon Ladies Association, which purchased the estate for $200,000 in 1858. There was a chance of the estate crumbling if the ladies had not bought it.

New York Central Park

Central Park is situated in the middle of Manhattan and this is the most famous of the city's hundred parks. This vast recreational site is 2 ½ miles long and ½ mile wide. This beloved stretch of greenery designed by Olmsted and Vaux in the 1860s is a national historic landmark. New Yorkers use it for everything—jogging, biking, walking, ice-skating, riding in horse drawn hansoms, listening to concerts and operas, watching Shakespearean plays, flying kites, boating and playing all types of ball games. The park covers an area of 840 acres and took 20 years to implement. It has a bird sanctuary, lakes, ponds, bridle paths, walks and park drives. There is a famous Egyptian Obelisk called 'Cleopatra's Needle'. Also, there is a huge open air theatre. The park has been the scene of several American plays and films.

United Nations

This working monument to world peace is located in the midst of New York City. Yet it is not a part of America, but an international area bound by its own laws. The UN headquarters occupies 18 acres of international territory—neither the city nor the US has jurisdiction over it. It was designed by an international team of architects, which was led by an American, Wallace Harrison and included La Corbusier, who designed our Chandigarh. A 39 storey glass slab Secretariat adjoins the main building, which houses the General Assembly. It is located on beautifully landscaped grounds donated by John D. Rockefeller Jr. Over 190 nations use the facilities to arbitrate worldwide disputes.

Guided tours take us to the General Assembly Hall and the Security Council chamber and introduce us to the history and activities of the UN and its related organisations. Along the tour, we see donated objects and artwork as also charred artifacts from the atomic bombs at Hiroshima and Nagasaki, stained glass windows by Chagall, a replica of the first Sputnik and a colourful mosaic called 'The Golden Rule' based on a Norman Rockwell drawing gifted by the US.

In the foyer, paintings from children all over the world are displayed and we were very happy to see on display the painting by a 10 year old girl from India—Anjali Chandrasekhar. Her subject was 'Pollution'. In the Security Council, we were allowed to sit in the visitor's gallery and my mind went back to the stirring speeches of V.K. Krishna Menon, which combined eloquence with power. Adjoining the river is a lawn, which contains the beautiful statue of a sword being turned into a ploughshare.

American Museum of Natural History

The $210 million Rose Center for Earth and Space has a four storey tall Planetarium Sphere, which hosts the excellent space show 'Are We Alone?', the most technologically advanced space show on earth. Its narration is by Harrison Ford. Prepare to be blown away. The show is for a half-hour, but phenomenal it is. It was rightly called 'The World's largest most powerful virtual-reality stimulator.' A big-bang theatre recreates the birth of the universe. The main hall of the universe has a 15 ½ tonne meteorite. The hall of planet earth focusses on the geological growth of our planet. The diversity of the building's holdings is astounding—some 36 million specimen ranging from microscopic organisms to the world's largest cut gem, the Brazilian 'Princess Topaz', all of 21,500 carats.

There was a special exhibition on 'Sikh Religion' when we visited. As we entered the Hall, we could hear *gurbani*. The history of Sikhism was brought out by display of paintings and authentic artifacts brought from India. A miniature Golden Temple lends authority to the exhibition.

Times Square, NASDAQ and Wall Street

The crowds at 'The Times Square' are thicker than the one in Mumbai, and one has a distinctly stifling feeling here. There are lots of restaurants, shops and the inevitable 'Broadway'. Shows here cost a fortune, but are worth a *dekko*. We saw 'Lion King' with exotic music by Sir Elton John. When we emerged from the theatre, it was past 11 pm and an entirely different world was what we entered into. Life size and giant ads scream at you for attention—Coca Cola, Pepsi Cola, Nokia, Hyundai, and Honda etc. You walk a few minutes into the famous 'Wall Street', the world's prime hub for bulls and bears. This narrow 18th century lane is lined with neo-classical towers that reach as far skywards as the dreams and greed of investors, who built it into the world's most famous financial market. At the heart of the action is the 'NYSE'—the New York Stock Exchange, which is not open to public. About 3,000 companies are currently listed on the exchange and trading of over 314 million shares takes place at an estimated value of $16 trillion. Broad illuminated bands scream into the night—the Dow-Jones indices and the latest quotes of stocks and shares. A paradise for investors. Or is it hell? One wonders.

TRAVELS »

26 Travels in Europe

Paris

We left Sahar Airport in the tiny hours of May 7 and landed at Abu Dhabi Airport. Here a ghastly thing occurred. Our group of 80 was split into two and different buses took us to different hotels. The ladies were herded into one bus, and separated from them and put in another bus were their husbands. This reminded me of the scenes in Schindler's list, where the Gestapo forcibly divided families and sent the women to one concentration camp and the men to another. Our ladies were warned that they must guard their passports, their *mangal sutras*, and what happened was that they were separated from those who had put *mangal sutras* on them. Horror was to follow when the hotel authorities took away their passports. Thus, the tour started with near panic for some. Wives divided from husbands and passports taken away. Happily, the next morning, what was put together by God and torn asunder by man was rejoined. From Abu Dhabi we flew to Paris, the capital of France.

Paris is situated on the river Seine and has a population of over 2 million. It is a major influence in politics, fashion, business, science and arts. Paris has many names but the most popular is 'The City of Light', chiefly because it is the centre of education and also for its early adoption of street lightning. Paris was the centrestage for the French Revolution with the storming of the Bastille in 1789. The city underwent a massive renovation under Hausmann, who created the neo-classical facades of modern Paris. Paris hosted the Universal

Exposition, and the Eiffel Tower was built for the centennial of the French Revolution. The city was home to artists like Stravinsky, Picasso, Dali and Hemingway. Paris came under German occupation during 1940 till it was liberated. Hitler had ordered that all French monuments must be destroyed before the German retreat, but Gen Von Choltitz disobeyed him.

We walked along the Champs de Elysees, which is the most beautiful avenue in the world. It is a 17th century garden promenade with a major shopping street and connects the Arc de Triomphe and the Place de la Concorde. The latter is the site of the infamous 'Guillotine' that chopped off several royal heads, as also of the man who was responsible for it—Robespierre. We saw here the oldest monument in Paris—the Egyptian Obelisk.

We cruised on the Seine River by night, and saw the original Statue of Liberty and several office buildings and palaces of three centuries standing and the stunning sight of the illuminated Eiffel Tower. The next day was dedicated to Euro-Disney, the Louvre Museum, the Arc de Triomphe and the Eiffel Tower. Euro-Disney is a major tourist attraction and is a copy of the original one in California.

We assembled at the base of the inverted glass pyramid at the entrance to the Louvre Museum. Readers of the 'Da Vinci Code' will recall that the novel starts here. The Louvre Museum houses many works of art, but the most famous is 'Mona Lisa', the great painting of Leonardo Da Vinci, who was the greatest man who ever lived. He was sculptor, painter, scientist, poet and man of several parts. He could write at the same time with both right hand and left hand on two subjects. He gave an accurate chart of human anatomy and made a model of a helicopter as we know it today. Leonardo started painting the 'Mona Lisa' in 1506 and took four years to complete. The title means Madam Lisa— Mona being a contraction of Madonna. The model is identified as the wife of a Florentine businessman. Louis XIV moved the painting to his palace at Versailles and Napoleon kept it in his bedroom. It was stolen in 1911 and was hidden in an Italian attic for two years. A Louvre employee Vincenzo Peruggia stole it and tried to sell it when he was caught. Now the painting is covered with a bullet proof security glass and it is insured for 60 million US dollars. It is notable that Mona Lisa has no visible facial hair—including eye brows and eye lashes.

After the Louvre we went on to see the Arc de Triomphe, a monument in the centre of Place Charles de Gaulle—designed by Jean Chalgrin in 1806. The monument is 165 feet in height and is 150 feet wide. It is the second largest triumphal arch in existence, and an early daredevil—Charles Godefroy—flew his plane through it. Commissioned by Napoleon, it was completed after his death only in 1836. The inside walls list the names of 558 generals. Beneath the arc is the tomb of the unknown soldier.

We spent the entire evening at the Eiffel Tower. It is one of the tallest structures in Paris—1,063 feet in height including the 78 feet antenna. In 1902 it was struck by lightning, which meant that 100 metres of the top had to be reconstructed. Till 1930, when the Chrysler Building was completed, the Eiffel was the tallest monument in the world. The Eiffel Tower weighs 7,300 tonnes. There are 1,665 steps and the tower sways 6-7 cms in the wind. The tower was built to commemorate the centenary of the French Revolution. Eiffel planned to build it in Barcelona, but the Spanish government rejected it. There was only one death during construction. Eiffel had a permit for the tower for 20 years only, but it continued as it was valuable for communication purposes. Wireless signals were exchanged between the Eiffel and the US Naval Observatory. During the German occupation of France, it was used to telecast German TV broadcasts. Since 1957 the tower has been used for regular transmission of FM and television. From 1925 to 1934, illuminated signs for Citroen adorned the tower's four sides, making it the tallest billboard in the world then. On the top of the tower the names of 72 scientists, engineers and some other notable people are engraved, in recognition of their contributions. There were many who did not approve of the tower—including Tolstoy and Guy Maupassant. Maupassant ate everyday in the restaurant in the tower (there are two, in fact). Asked why he came, he said, "That is the only place in Paris from where you cannot see the wretched tower."

One of the star attractions was a visit to the 'French Lido'. It is a cabaret and burlesque house on the Champs de Elysees, famous for its exotic shows, which rival those of Las Vegas. On the night we went, the show started at 10 pm and went on till 12 in the night. Champagne was served free, and for timid Indians like me there was orange juice. The staggering item for most of us was the female artists who were bare breasted and gambolled vigorously with athletic men. The stage was in the middle and we sat around it. From where I sat, we could shake hand with the artists—if we wished. Of the women on the stage, even the nipples were visible—with bottoms and bosoms in abundance! While the men of our group were ogling shamelessly, their wives were stupefied with embarrassment! A memorable item of our visit to the great entertainment capital of Europe!

En route we saw the tunnel in which Lady Diana and Dodi Fayed crashed to their death. The Princess and Fayed departed on August 30, 1997 from the Hotel Ritz in Place Vendome and sped along the Seine. At midnight, their Mercedes Benz entered the underpass below the Place de Palma travelling at great speed chased by nine French photographers on motorcycles. The car lost control and collided with the 13th pillar—instead of rescuing the injured, the paparazzi were taking photos. The rest is history.

Florence

We entered the state of Italy through the Mont Blanc tunnel, which is one of the major trans-alpine transport routes. Begun in 1957 and completed in 1965, the tunnel is 7.25 miles long, 28.2 feet wide and 14.3 feet high. The tunnel is not vertical, but an inverted 'V'. Altitude on the French side is 4,091 feet and on the Italian side 4,530 feet. On March 29, 1999, 39 people died when a Belgian truck carrying margarine and flour caught fire in the tunnel. We saw a monument at the entrance to the tunnel on the French side dedicated to those who lost their lives. Mont Blanc has another significance for us as it was here that the Father of Indian nuclear programme, Dr Homi Bhabha perished in an air crash -'Kanchenjunga' in 1966.

En route to Italy, we had a brief halt at Geneva and saw Lake Geneva with the tallest fountain in the world exactly in the middle of the lake. The 'Jet de Eau', which commenced functioning in 1886 is 140 metres high and is quite an impressive sight. We also saw—from our bus—a bit of Geneva—the offices of United Nations and other International agencies as also, the airport at Geneva. Incidentally, this airport closes down daily at 8 pm. No planes land or take off after that. My companion in the present trip was stuck up at this airport the entire night!

From Geneva we were to proceed to Pisa—the nearest touring spot but did not, as an International Cycle Race was being held in Pisa and it was out of bounds for tourists. So we proceeded to that seat of culture, the source of European cultural efflorescence—Florence or Firenze as it is known. Read the names of a few Florentines and you will realise the greatness of the place we were to see next: Dante, Boccacio, Michelangelo, the Medici family, Raphael, Leonardo Da Vinci, Galileo, Niccolo Machiavelli, Donatello and the universally revered Florence Nightingale. Such a massive contribution these great people had made that Florence is rightly called the Cradle of Western Civilisation, as we know it. Firenze is the capital of the Tuscany region of Italy. It was also the capital of Italy from 1845 to 1870. Florence lies on the Arno River and has a population of 4 lakh. It is the birthplace of the Italian Renaissance and is noted for its magnificent art and architecture. It is said that, of the 1,000 most important European artists of the second millennium, 350 lived or worked in Florence. United Nations Educational Scientific and Cultural Organisation (UNESCO) declared Florence a World Heritage Site in 1982.

The most important family in Florence was the Medici family, and Cosimo de Medici became a banker to the Popes. Lorenzo, his grandson was a great patron of arts and commissioned the works of Michelangelo, Leonardo da Vinci and Botticelli. Niccolo Machiavelli was a noted political thinker whose 'Prince' is a latter-day-version of Kautilya's 'Arthasastra'. We went to the house in which Dante was born and the church in which he prayed.

A bit of details about two of the greatest artists in history Leonardo da Vinci (1452-1519) was a polymath, scientist, mathematician, engineer, inventor, anatomist, painter, sculptor, architect, writer and musician. Two of his paintings, the 'Mona Lisa' and the 'Last Supper' occupy unique position as two of the most famous paintings of all time. He conceptually invented a helicopter, a tank, a calculator. He greatly advanced knowledge of anatomy, optics and study of water. The original of one of his books 'Codex Leicester' is with Bill Gates.

Michelangelo Buonarroti (1475-1564) was actually a sculptor, who at the young age of 23 carved that marvellously moving statue 'Pieta', which is in St Peter's Basilica in Rome. This statue shows the dead Jesus Christ in the lap of Virgin Mary, and many shed tears and simply stand entranced before it! Another famous statue he carved was that of the young 'David'. But Michelangelo is rightly famous for his painting the ceiling of the Sistine Chapel in St Peter's. Pope Julius II ordered him to paint the ceiling of this chapel built by Pope Sixtus IV. Michelangelo painted on the ceiling, the ancestors of Christ, salvation of the Jews, David and Goliath, the prophets, Jonah and the whale. He started painting—standing—in 1505 and completed it in 1512. He wrote a satirical poem, complaining of stiff neck and paint dropping into his eyes. Prior to this, the ceiling was painted blue with stars. For film buffs, I commend 'The Agony and Ecstasy'—the book being authored by Irving Stone.

We got a panoramic view of Florence city from the Piazza Michelangelo with a stunningly beautiful statue of Michelangelo. The best known site and architectural jewel of Florence is the domed cathedral of the city, Santa Maria del Fiore, known as the Duomo. The magnificent dome was built by Brunelleschi. The work on the cathedral began in 1296 and was completed in 1436. Inside there are paintings of two mercenaries John Hawkwood and Nicolo Talentino. A painting by Michelangelo shows Dante with the cathedral itself in the background. This was painted in 1465. The cathedral is 153 metres long and 90 metres wide at the crossing.

The Arno River is a 'character' in Florentine history—alternately nourishing the city with commerce and destroying it with flood. The Ponte Vecchio is a unique old bridge with a number of shops built upon its edges, held up by stilts. The 'Uffuzi' had offices of government, and is now a museum outside which stood the original statue of David by Michelangelo. Now a substitute stands here. The original has been shifted indoors to the Accademia dell Arte del Designo. The Santa Croce church contains the tombs of Galileo, Michaelangelo, Machiavelli, Dante and many other notables—an Italian equivalent to Westminster Abbey.

Florence has been the background for many novels and films—to mention a few Hannibal, Tea with Mussolini and A Room with a View.

Our next halt is familiar to all of us through the famous play of William Shakespeare -'The Merchant of Venice'. Who has not heard of Shylock and Portia?

Venice and Pisa

As we wandered on the super smooth—as soft as a new-born baby's bum—Autobahn over vast areas of Europe, I used to provide daily information on the places we saw or were about to see. We had in our group—mainly Maharashtrians—a lawyer from Nasik, who declared that South Indians are good in English and Maharashtrians are not. I rejected his contention by stating that if he admired my English, I could assure him that I learnt English from my father in school and in college from Vinda Karandikar, Y.D. Phadke and Ram Joshi. Vinda, of course, bagged the Bharatiya Jnanpith Award. He translated King Lear into Marathi. It was, he who taught me Byron's 'Child Harolde's Pilgrimage' wherein comes the 'Bridge of Sighs', which we are about to see in Venice.

Venice or Venezia is the capital of the Veneto region and has a population of 271,663. It is called 'Queen of the Adriatic', 'City of Bridges' and 'City of Water'. The city stretches across numerous small islands in the marshy Venetian lagoon along the Adriatic Sea in north east Italy. The city was a flourishing trade centre between western Europe and the rest of the world. Venice became an Imperial power after the fourth Crusade when it seized Constantinople and brought considerable plunder including the winged Lion of St Mark—a symbol of Venice. During the 13th century, Venice was the most prosperous city in all of Europe. The city was governed by the Great Council made up of some of the influential families—the power of governance being vested in the Duke or 'Doge'. Napoleon conquered Venice in 1797 and it became Austrian territory for a while before reverting to Italy.

Venice is an archipelago of 122 islands, formed by about 150 canals. The islands on which the city is built are connected by 400 bridges. Every form of transport is on water or on foot. Venice is Europe's largest urban car-free area. The classical Venetian boat is the Gondola—wrongly pronounced by our guides from India as Gandola—despite my correcting them! The motorised waterbuses, which the Venetians use for transport are called the 'Vaporetti'.

St Mark's Square in the centre of the city was constructed in the 12th century in front of the Basilica—built for the Doge—but was used for events of a religious or political nature. The St Mark's Square has the biggest collection of pigeons I have seen. Since I carried some biscuits, I kept it in my hand and a dozen pigeons sat on my hands and pecked at the crumbs. There are two massive pillars—on top of one is the winged lion and on the other, St George slaying the dragon. Irving Wallace has a fascinating book based on Venice called 'The Pigeon Project', which is as readable as the 'Da Vinci Code'.

Another important monument I referred to earlier is the 'Bridge of Sighs'. It received its name in the 17th century because the prisoners who passed through this bridge on their way to the prison cells on the other side would see the beautiful sight of the lagoon and the island of Giorgio for the last time, and they would all sigh as they crossed this bridge. The buildings of Venice are constructed on closely spaced wood piles, which penetrate alternating layers of clay and sand. The buildings are often threatened by the flood from the Adriatic. There is a belief that the city is slowly sinking and the MOSE project is expected to ensure that it does not.

Venice appears in several books - Shakespeare's 'Merchant of Venice' and 'Othello', Thomas Mann's 'Death in Venice' and Hemingway's 'Across the River and Into the Trees'. Of course, most of us have seen Sean Connery in From Russia with Love, which featured Venice. Other films are Moonraker, Casino Royale—all Bond flicks and the eternally charming The Italian Job. The most famous Venetian was Marco Polo who went on an adventure up to China and is supposed to have helped in the engineering of the Brihadeeswara Temple at Thanjavur. On the northern tower of this magnificent temple, there is the figure of a foreigner in a top hat with a pipe in his mouth along with gods from our Pantheon. It is a tribute to Marco Polo.

Our next monument was the 'Leaning Tower of Pisa'—a wonderful structure. It is actually a campanile or bell tower of the cathedral at Pisa. Although intended to stand erect, the tower began to tilt soon after construction in 1173 due to poorly laid foundation and loose substrate. The tower deviates 16.9 feet from the perpendicular and moves down at the rate of 0.043 inch per year. The tower's height is 183.27 feet from the ground on the lower side and 186.02 feet on the higher side. The width of the wall at the base is 13.42 feet and 8.14 feet at the top. The tower is estimated to weigh 14,500 tonnes. It has 294 steps. It was constructed in three stages over a period of 174 years. Five centuries later, the tower is unscarred from the ravages of weather and age. The tower was the centre of an important experiment by Galileo, who is said to have carried two cannon balls of different masses and dropped them from the top of the tower to demonstrate that their descending speed was independent of their mass. Benito Mussolini ordered that the tower be returned to vertical position, but this experiment led to its further sinking into the ground. The tower was closed for almost 10 years from 1990 for repairs and it is believed that it will remain stable for the next 300 years. It is now a UNESCO World Heritage Site.

In the movie Superman III, an evil Superman straightens the tower and the real Superman pushes it back to its normal position.

We are now on the way to that pinnacle of human achievement—Rome. Since 'Rome was not built in a day' my write-up on 'Rome will not be written in a day' do look forward to a sweet Roman holiday.

Rome

Rome—the Eternal City, the City of Seven Hills, the city of 'Roman Holiday', where the most beautiful, elfin, fairy like Miss Audrey Hepburn captured the hearts of all and bagged the Oscar at 24. Rome—seat of the Popes, the riches of the Vatican, Rome of antiquity, in fact a dream world indeed! Rome or Roma, the capital of Italy with a population of 3.8 million is one of the largest cities of the European Union. According to legend, Rome was founded by the twins Romulus and Remus in 753 BC. (Romulus killed Remus just as Cain killed Abel). The city was the cradle of Roman civilisation that produced the longest empire of antiquity. Rome is identified with the Catholic church. An enclave of Rome is the State of Vatican City, the sovereign territory of the Holy See and the smallest nation in the world. Rome escaped World War II relatively unscathed. The historic centre of Rome is also a UNESCO World Heritage Site.

For almost a 1000 years, Rome was the most politically important, richest and largest city in the western world. With the decline of the empire, it lost its capital status to Milan and even Constantinople. Rome remained the capital of the Papal states until it became part of Italy in 1870. The city witnessed the rise of Fascism under Benito Mussolini, who declared a new empire and allied it with Nazi Germany. The end of the War saw the execution of Mussolini followed by a referendum abolishing monarchy in favour of the Italian Republic. Rome is unique in its containing two other sovereign states. One is the Holy See, the political entity that governs the Vatican. The other is the sovereign state of Malta.

The Bishop of Rome known as the Pope claimed supremacy over all bishops and all Christians on the basis that he is the successor to Saint

Peter upon whom Jesus built his church. Churches proliferated during the Renaissance, when the most notable churches were built including the St Peter's Basilica—the largest church in the world. The St Peter's Square with the Basilica was designed by Bernini. Here are the Vatican Library, the Vatican museums with the Sistine Chapel, the Raphael rooms and other important works of Leonardo da Vinci, Michelangelo, Botticelli and others. One of the symbols of Rome is the Coliseum, the largest amphitheatre, capable of seating 50,000 spectators; it was used for gladiatorial fights. There is also the impressive Forum. The river that runs through Rome is the 'Tiber'.

One of the most impressive and lovable monuments is the 'Fountain de Trevi'. This fountain is named after the Virgin Mother. Water springs were built in Roman times and the fountain was restored by Albert under Pope Nicolo V, who also fixed the aqueduct. This meant that the Romans did not have to depend on the Tiber River. In 1650, Pope Urban VII hired Bernini for making some embellishments. In order to pay the artist he imposed a wine tax. We saw in the Louvre Museum a painting of Jesus converting water into wine. Here was a Pope who converted wine into water! It is believed that those who drop coins in this fountain have their wishes fulfilled and are also ensured a return to Rome. The annexed 'Fountain of Lovers' on the left side has a legend that those who drink water from it will stay faithful forever.

We saw en route the impressive Victor Emmanuel II Monument, built to commemorate the 50th anniversary of Italian unification. Victor Emmanuel, along with Cavour and Garibaldi, was responsible for Italian unification. Just near this, we viewed the drab palace of Benito Mussolini, the fascist dictator, who was executed by the public and whose body was hanged in a public square upside down! To more pleasant things now! The St Peter's Basilica is the most prominent building in the Vatican with an impressive dome. It has a capacity of 60,000 people. St Peter lies buried here as also many other Popes. Most papal ceremonies take place here due to its size and its proximity to the papal residence and location. There are over 100 tombs in the Basilica, including those of 91 Popes, the latest being John Paul II. St

Peter's Square built by Bernini between 1656 and 1667 is surrounded by a colonnade. In the centre is the Egyptian Obelisk, 131 feet high. The dome was designed by Michelangelo. The façade is 376 feet wide and 149 feet high. The statues of St Peter and St Paul are in front of the parish. The northern most door called the 'Holy Door' is opened only for jubilee years. Walking along the right aisle, we saw the 'Pieta' of Michelangelo. The representation of a chair, part of a sculpture, is said to be the remnants of the chair belonging to St Peter. We were singularly unlucky in not being able to see the Sistine chapel. This is the official residence of the Pope. It is known for its architecture, frescoes and painting. The ceiling was painted by Michelangelo who took four years to complete it. He stood and painted the ceiling. The paintings were on God's creation of the world, God's relationship with man, and mankind's fall from grace. The wall above the altar has 'The Last Judgment' of Michelangelo. For book lovers I warmly commend 'The Agony and Ecstasy' by Irving Stone. It is also in the Sistine Chapel that the Papal conclave selects the new Pope. Look forward to some good Pope stories.

After admiring the Basilica, we went to the Coliseum, a giant amphitheatre that can accommodate about 50,000 spectators. It was used for gladiatorial contests between lions and slaves. It was completed in 80 AD and remained in use for 500 years. Though it is in ruins now, it is seen as a symbol of Imperial Rome and is one of the finest examples of Roman architecture. Each 'Good Friday' the Pope leads a 'Way of Cross' procession to the Coliseum.

In the St Peter's Basilica we saw the embalmed body of Pope John XXIII. He was known as 'Good Pope John' as he was the most liberal Pope who allowed prayers to be said in local languages and not in Latin. He liberated the community from several constraints. He was a man with a great sense of humour. Physically he was like a Sumo wrestler—huge and he succeeded Pius XII who was a frail, slim man. One story is that immediately after his elevation to papacy he enquired about the salary paid to the porters, who bear him on his *sedia* (chair). When the officials enquired why he wanted to know he said, "Well, they should get a hefty rise in salary as the weight of the Pope has doubled!" An eminent Canadian photographer Yousuf Karsh of Ottawa who visited the Pope was invited by His Holiness to accompany him on a morning walk in the papal garden. He asked—to make a little conversation, "How many people work in the Vatican?" His Holiness smiled and said "Half of them."

Innsbruck and Lucerne

It is averred that when Shankaracharya went to Benares for his famous controversy with the Mimamsa scholar Mandana Mishra, he enquired of the house where the latter stayed. He was told, "You will find in the courtyard of that house parrots will be discussing high principles of philosophy." As we entered Austria, I was reminded of this as every bird or animal or human being in Austria is a composer, and music found its best expression here. Vienna is the cultural capital of Austria. Mozart, Haydn, Schubert, Bruckner and Strauss, and a number of other composers were born here and poured out their melody in abundance. Austria means culture at its best.

What a scenic beauty as we traverse from Italy to Austria! Austria is a land locked mountainous country as it is located in the Alps. It is noted for its picturesque Alpine villages. If you have seen the movie Sound of Music and recall the rolling plains in which Julie Andrews dances and sings—this is the scene all over Austria. Dripping with beauty, tiny chalets evenly spaced out cling to the high cliffs, cows and buffaloes grazing in their hundreds, a charming scene of lush greenery for miles on end, innumerable waterfalls—scenes that will cool your eyes and soothe your hearts.

Austria, a parliamentary democracy made up of nine states, has declared itself to be a permanently neutral country. Earlier the most important dynasty was that of the Habsburgs whose Empress Maria Theresa aligned herself with Bourbons by arranging the wedding of her daughter Marie Antoinette with the French King. During the last century, the First World War is said to have begun with the assassination of the Archduke Ferdinand on June 28, 1914 in

Sarajevo. German troops of Hitler marched into Austria in 1938. He established a concentration camp here. Austria, which became independent in 1955 has a population of 8.29 million people. One of the nine states is Tyrol of which the capital is Innsbruck. We entered Austria through Innsbruck, with a population of 117,287. It is an important tourist and winter sports resort, and hosted the 1964 and 1976 Winter Olympics. The bridge over the river Inn, which gives the city its name, has made Innsbruck an important point on the trade route from Germany to Switzerland and Italy. In the morning, we visited the 'Golden Roof' where the Empress Maria Theresa used to give audiences to the public.

The evening was spent in the magic crystal world of 'Swarovski'. On entering the large, blue entrance hall, you see the world in new ways. You can watch sparkling crystal artworks of famous artists such as Salvador Dali, Andy Warhol. In the centre is the 'Centenar', the largest cut crystal in the world—310,000 carats. Quite exciting is the 42 metre long and 11 metre high crystal wall filled with 12 tonnes of glittering crystals.

After a most satisfying Austrian holiday, we enter an enchanting country—Switzerland. Another landlocked country with 7.5 million people, it has 26 cantons. It has a long history of being neutral and has not been in any war since 1815 and thus, hosts various international organisations such as the UN. The international Red Cross was founded here. Swiss constitution has an emphasis on direct democracy. Two world wars did not touch Switzerland. The country gave asylum to Lenin, who remained here from 1917 to 1920. Women were granted rights to vote only in 1959. Today the President is a woman. In 2002, Switzerland became a full-fledged member of the UN leaving the Vatican as the only non-recognised member of the UN.

The country rejected membership of the European Union through a referendum in 1992. This was the only country where we had to convert our Euros into Swiss francs. Switzerland has 26 cantons, the most important of which are Basel, Berne, Lucerne and Zurich. Several major rivers such as the Rhine, Rhone and Inn flow into the Geneva

Lake. The most famous mountain is the Matterhorn. The section of the Bernese Alps above the deep glacial Lauterbrunnen Valley contains 72 waterfalls and is well known for the Jungfrau, Monch and Eiger peaks. The Swiss are well known for their affinity for cleanliness and punctuality. They have one of the best road and public transportation systems in the world.

Since we stayed in Lucerne we saw the 'Kappelbrucke' on the shore of Lake Lucerne. It means the bridge leading to the chapel. We saw and walked through a 14th century wooden bridge, 677 feet long and constructed in 1333. It was rebuilt after a fire in 1933. Inside the bridge are paintings of 17th century, depicting events from Lucerne's history. The bridge leads you on to an ancient chapel.

A moving monument is the 'Lion Monument'—a famous carving by a Danish artist Bertel Thorvaldsen of a dying lion commemorating the murder of hundreds of Swiss guards in the French Revolution. The Swiss officers were guarding King Louis XIV and Marie Antoinette and the Dauphin. A mob stormed the palace and killed all the Swiss guards. The lion was carved out of rock and Mark Twain called it—"The saddest and most moving piece of rock in the world". You will feel the sadness of the lion in its face and empathise with it. The monument depicts a dying lion over a Swiss shield with a spear protruding from its side.

Some of the famous Swiss people are Le Corbusier, Ursula Andress, George Piaget, Jean Jacques Roussaeu and Henri Dunant. Of course all of us know about Corbusier, who designed Chandigarh City. He also designed the UN building in New York. A line about Swiss bank secrecy will be essential. Swiss banks are under obligation to keep all accounts strictly secret. Any banker who reveals information without the client's permission will be jailed. Exceptions are gun-running and smuggling. Bank secrecy is not lifted even for tax evasion. In a referendum in 1983, 73 per cent voted for secrecy. All accounts are numbered. In all documents, only a number appears. Very few people know the identity of clients. Sanjay Gandhi and Ottavio Quattrocchi have stashed their ill gotten funds here in Zurich, as also the dictators of South America—the bankers here are called the Gnomes of Zurich. You can know a lot about Swiss banks if you read Jeffrey Archer's 'A Matter of Honour' or Dan Brown's 'Da Vinci Code'. Happy reading! We will venture into the Swiss Alps—Mount Titlis and the highest railway station in the world Jungfrau—next.

Mt Titlis and Jungfrau

Mount Titlis at 3,020 metres above sea level is the loftiest accessible peak of Switzerland. It has the world's first revolving cable car called Rotair and we enjoyed breathtaking views of the Alps. The cable car provides a 360 degree panoramic view of the snow-covered valleys, glaciers, Black Forest region, lakes and mountains. We get to the top by three different aerial cable cars through many changes of scenery from the green valley up into the high alpine glacier region in almost 50 minutes. About 200 cable cars with flags of different nations take you to a station midway. Cable car no. 73 carries the Indian flag—our Tricolour. The Mount Titlis station is at a height of 10,000 feet and one walks on a glacier. In the heart of the Titlis glacier, they have created a glacier cave. You are surrounded by sparkling walls of ice. 8,450 lights infuse colour to the cave and transform it into a special atmosphere. Unexpected sounds contribute to a unique impression. A truly memorable experience!

Our next experience out of this world was the climb up to Jungfrau (meaning 'Virgin'), the highest peak of a mountain mastiff of the same name located in the Bernese region of the Alps overlooking Wengen. The other two peaks here are the Eiger and the Monch. Once difficult to access, the Jungfraubahn cog railway now runs inside the mountain up to the Jungfraujoch railway station—at 11,333 feet—the highest station in the world. We commence our upward journey from Lauterbrunnen. Here is the stunning Stubach Falls, which inspired Goethe to pen his 'Song of the Spirits over the Waters'. When we reach Kleine Scheidegg, we changed over to another train. That train runs close behind the Eiger's north face, stopping at Eigerwand, where there is a window about eight metres long and one metre high. This window is used as access points to rescue climbers. For the ordinary man, it acts as platform from which photographs of the grand view can be taken. There is a second stop and a second window looking out on the Eismeer—the sea of ice—before the train continues its journey. The tunnel was constructed between 1898 and 1912, and it is about 7 kms long with gradient of up to 25 per cent. The upward journey takes 50 minutes with two stops and the return journey only 35 minutes. At the top there are two restaurants, an observatory, a research station and the 'Ice Palace', which has an elaborate collection of ice sculptures. One can walk out on a flat surface covered by solid snow and view the Aletsch glacier.

After these eerie experiences, we went back to the drive over the Autobahn now traversing the 'Black Forest' in the southwest grape vineyards. The valleys are fertile and make good pasture land for grape vineyards. Lumbering, woodworking and the manufacture of toys and cuckoo clocks are the main industries. On the way we halted at the famous Rhine Falls—the largest waterfall in Europe on the Rhine river. Amazingly, here we got *vada pav* and *samosa—garam garam*! Maharashtrian pride swelled as also Indian bellies! A cook from Rajasthan has made a lot of Euros here catering such food. Black Forest is of course where cuckoo clocks are made—it is also famous for Black Forest cakes. We halted at Hofgut Sternen whose history started 600 years ago and its greatest hour was when Marie Antoinette daughter of Maria Theresa, passed through the Hollental on her way to Paris to marry the King of France. Her marriage procession halted in the grounds of this Inn and it was a sight to be seen. Famous guests included Goethe and Napoleon III. The Drubba family, which makes the cuckoo clock is world famous and we were shown how the clock is made. The first cuckoo clock was made in 1640. We acquired a cuckoo clock.

Our next halt was Cologne. It is Germany's fourth largest city and lies on the west bank of the Rhine river. The Cologne Cathedral is the star attraction after its Eau-de Cologne. Cologne was heavily bombed during the Second World War. 20,000 civilians were killed and the centre of the city was completely destroyed. It has been reconstructed.

The Gothic Cologne Cathedral—with its twin spires reaching up to 515 feet—was begun in 1248 and completed in 1880. It is called 'Eternal Construction Site', and throughout the year some work or other goes on this cathedral. There is a belief that the world will come to an end once construction stops.

Our next halt is Netherlands followed by Belgium when we bid adieu to Europe and then we go to London—home of Shakespeare.

Netherlands and Belgium

Netherlands or Holland is famous for Dutch courage and Dutch parsimony. It is a constitutional monarchy, densely populated (15 million) and known for its windmills, cheese, clogs, dykes, tulips and extremely liberal social policies—euthanasia is allowed officially. Interpol headquarters and International Court of Justice are located here at Hague. After freeing themselves from Spanish rule, the Dutch became one of the great seafaring and economic powers of 17th century. Amsterdam became the wealthiest trading city of the world and the first stock exchange was started here. Indonesia and Suriname were some of the colonies of Holland. Germany overran Holland during world war and Jews were sent to concentration camps. The country was the founder member of NATO and Benelux, and today it is part of the European Union. Queen Beatrix is the present monarch.

A remarkable feature of Netherlands is that it is a flat country, and half the surface is under sea level. An extensive range of dykes and dunes protect these areas from flooding. A substantial part of the country is reclaimed from the sea. Netherlands is called 'A land won from the sea'. It is said that God created the world, but the Dutch created Netherlands. Amsterdam, Hague, and Rotterdam are the major cities. Netherlands had many great painters—Rembrandt, Vermeer, Vincent van Gogh. The philosophers Erasmus and Spinoza were born here. Amsterdam was founded by two fishermen and a dog. The river Amstel was dammed and thus we got the Amsterdam. During Second World War Hitler invaded Holland, and over one lakh Jews were sent to concentration camps. The most famous was a young girl Anne Frank who wrote a dairy while hiding in the loft of her father's office. She was discovered and sent to Belsen where she died. Her book 'The Dairy of a Young Girl' is a moving document and has been filmed. There is an Anne Frank Museum here. The original dairy is on display in the museum.

Amsterdam has six lakh bicycles. Windmills are so popular that there is a Windmill Day—May 11th every year. There were 10,000 windmills in the 18th century as against only 1,000 today. On the Queen's birthday, the city turns orange as Orange is the name of the current dynasty. Royalty mixes freely with public. Queen Beatrix can be found standing in a queue in a mall waiting for her turn to pay the bill!

The highlight of our tour here was the famous Tulip Gardens at Keukenhof. We saw it by sheer chance as it was closed for public that very evening. This was the scene of the famous Amitabh-Rekha starrer Silsila. Keukenhof means 'Kitchen Garden' and from 1406 to 1436, it was the estate of Countess Jacoba Von Bayern. She gathered herbs from the Castle's kitchen and hence, the name stuck. Keukenhof Park was designed by Zucher—father and son. The flower garden itself was inaugurated in 1949 by the Mayor of Lisse—Mr Lambooy. The garden is rich in both flora and fauna. There are 30 types of birds here. We were deluged by tulips of all colours. You will be spell bound at the sight of beautiful display of over seven million tulips, daffodils, narcissi and other flowers spread over 80 acres.

After drinking deep flowers we went to Madurodam, which is a Dutch city in miniature. Objects are made on scale of 1:25. There are 167 models including Schipol Airport, Dutch Parliament, and Royal Palace etc. Madurodam opened in July 1952—is named after George Maduro who was killed in World War II at the age of 29. His parents wished to erect a monument to him. At the same time, the Dutch Student Sanatorium Foundation sought funds to support youth oriented charities. Princess Beatrix was the first Mayor of this city in miniature. A council consisting of school children from Hague appoints the Mayor.

At the age of six, I was taught English in my school by a teacher Miss Thomas—a winsome, dainty Keralite lady always smelling of fresh roses! The smell still lingers—she taught us the story of a Dutch boy who on the way home from school finds that a hole has been formed in the dyke and had to be filled in. So he climbed up and the whole night, he stayed with his finger in the hole till those in search of him found him in the morning. He had saved the country from flooding. A story of Dutch courage! But she had not told the name of the boy. At Madurodam, at the entrance, there is a full size sculpture of the boy saving the country with his finger stopping the water. His name is given as Hansje Brinker. I have waited 65 years to know the boy's name. I recalled my teacher and thanked her. We had in the late 60s a wonderfully entertaining Hollywood movie If it is Tuesday, this must be Belgium, a romantic comedy directed by Mel Stuart, starring Suzanne Pleshette. The plot was based on a whirlwind tour of Europe like ours. As in the film—by serendipity—we arrived in Belgium on a Tuesday! Belgium has a population of 10.5 million. It was a prosperous centre of commerce till 17th century, till it became a battlefield of Europe. Napoleon was defeated here in Waterloo by the Duke of Wellington. Belgium had acquired a lot of colonies in Africa. It is a constitutional monarchy and a democratic country. Voting is compulsory. The present monarch is King Albert II.

We went to see the most popular statue of Manneken Pis—of a small boy pissing into a fountain basin. En route to this is Belgium's tribute to Spain. There are impressive statues of Don Quixote and Sancho Panza, the former tilting at windmills. Of course, it is based on the novel 'Adventures of Don Quixote' by Miguei de Cervantes—the first ever comic novel in world literature written in 1605. Of course, Belgium is famous for that great comic hero 'Tin Tin' and Agatha Christie's detective 'Hercule Poirot'. We saw the Atomium—a remnant of the World Exposition of 1998. It is a structure representing concept of an iron molecule enlarged 165 billion times. There are nine globes arranged in the form of an iron molecule's structure. Research is conducted in several disciplines in each of the globes. Brussels hosted the famous Solvay conference, which was attended by Einstein,

Planck, Curie, Dirac, Bohr, Schrodinger, Heisenberg and others. At this conference, they discussed the New Quantum Theory. Out of the 29 scientists who took part, 17 had won Nobel Prizes.

We saw a bit of the business district Antwerp—centre of diamond trade and went to the Brussels station to board the Euro Star to travel under the English Channel—the Chunnel—to arrive in Waterloo, London.

England

We boarded at Brussels station, the internationally famous Euro star rail, which would take us to London by the Chunnel—the tunnel under the English Channel. It was no great shakes except that it is below the sea for about 11 kms. We crossed over from the continent to the pastoral village atmosphere of England, which William Shakespeare described in King Richard II as:

"This blessed plot, this earth, this realm, this England"

Since all of us are familiar with English history, I am not going to waste anyone's time recounting it. The English ruled us for centuries, terrorised us, humiliated us, impoverished the country and did a thousand evil things, but I do believe all this is nullified by the fact that they gave us the English language. They gave us Shakespeare, Milton, Keats, Byron, Scott, Dickens, Shelley, Wells, Shaw, Austen, Bronte, Hardy and scores of other good writers, who took us on a voyage of discovery and enlightenment and freedom.

In London we went to the Wax Museum of Madame Tussaud. Our group went ga ga over the latest addition of Shah Rukh Khan and had themselves snapped with him as well as Aishwarya Rai. A story I heard was that when Aishwarya Rai went for the opening of her wax model, a pressmen who had come asked the organisers, "Which is the wax model?" The live one did look like a wax woman!

Apart from the impressive individual items, Tussaud's had a new item. You are taken in a trolley for about half an hour. On both sides are recreated scenes from British history during the last 500 years. The Black Plague, the beheadings during reign of Henry VIII, the bombing of London by V2 rockets and several memorable events are brought to you very authentically with sound and light effects. A tour de force indeed! The visit to Tussaud's was followed by the visit to the Tower of London, where the Crown Jewels were held in absolute security. Indians were thrilled to see the Kohinoor diamond in the crown of the Queen Mother. We were told by the guide that only seven executions have taken place in the tower, including that of Jane Seymour, only 17. I chided her for not revealing that just outside, in the grounds 110 people were executed! Inside the tower, at one spot, there are a dozen ravens or crows. There is a belief that if the ravens vanish, the tower and the surroundings will also collapse. So the ravens are well taken care of!

This was followed by a visit to Buckingham Palace, where we saw the impressively attired Queen's guards. Some visitors to the Queen came in cars and we found that all were asked to get down and everyone was subject to vigorous check. Fear has gripped England as it has the United States! Fear is the key.

The next day we went on a London city tour and saw Hyde Park, Nelson's Column, Houses of Parliament, Big Ben and No.10, Downing Street. We also went on the London Eye, a giant wheel, which turns round once in 30 minutes. One can see the entire city of London.

From Holiday Inn in Aylesbury to Stratford-upon-Avon was a two hour ride on a beautiful landscape with rolling plains and greenery as far as you can see. The damp British weather turned pleasant as worshippers of the Bard of Avon had come from the land of Kalidasa and Kamban. We reached Shakespeare's birthplace at 11 am. The cottage in which he was born is preserved in pristine purity. As we enter we see 38 plaques giving the names of his 38 plays. On exhibition are rare paintings of his times. His father's implements for making gloves are displayed. The bed in which Shakespeare was born is preserved. There was an attempt by Barnum—the Circus owner of USA—to buy the entire house and ship it to USA. It was resolutely opposed by a committee formed to protect England's greatest legacy and Charles Dickens played a leading part in this. A bit of Shakespeare for the uninitiated!

William Shakespeare was born on April 26, 1564 and died on April 23, 1616. Fifty-two years in all—the greatest writer of the English Language and pre-eminent dramatist of the world, he wrote 38 plays and 154 sonnets as also some poems. He is the national poet known as the 'Bard of Avon'. His works have been translated into several languages and we have the Marathi translation of King Lear by Vinda Karandikar. He was the son of John Shakespeare, a glove maker and Mary Arden. At the age of 18, he married Anne Hathaway who was 26—his senior by 8 years. Her cottage at Shattery—nearby is also well maintained. They had three children. Shakespeare himself was an actor. There are no direct descendants of Shakespeare alive today. There are speculations about the authorship of Shakespeare's works. Some believe Roger Bacon or Christopher Marlowe wrote the plays.

His plays were staged in the Globe Theatre, which was burnt down a few years ago. But the British built it again and even today, it is as it was in the Bard's time.

All over the world, several authorities sprang up on Shakespeare. India too has some authorities on the poet. The foremost was Prof Bradley. Students used to get Bradley by heart and then only face their examiners. There is an interesting story with which I conclude my piece on Shakespeare. The poor Bard had to sit for an exam on Shakespeare.

"Last night I dreamt that Shakespeare's ghost
sat for the Civil Service Post.
The question that year
Had several questions on King Lear.
Shakespeare answered very badly
Because he had not read Bradley."

27 Travels in India

Ashtavinayak Temples

Lord Ganesha has a special and exalted place in the Hindu pantheon of Gods. For success in all endeavours, his name has to be invoked at the very beginning. He is the remover of obstacles, and one who ensures success: *Sukha harta dukh harta*. Even his father Lord Shiva could not succeed in defeating the demon Tripurasura as he had forgotten to invoke the name of Ganesha.

In South India there are six houses of Ganesha's younger brother Karthikeya called 'Aru Padai Veedu'. Similarly there are eight houses of Ganesha located in and around Pune and these are known as 'Ashta Vinayaka Temples'. They are located at Ozar, Lenyadri, Mahad, Pali, Theur, Morgaon, Siddhatek and Ranjangaon. The temples are at a distance varying from 23 to 110 kms from Pune city. Excellent arrangements are available to visit the temples in two days. I shall deal with the temples as we covered them.

Sri Vigneshwara of Ozar

Abhinandana, a king at Hemawati was consumed by ambition and decided to perform a *yagna* that would lead him to victory over Indra, the Lord of heavens. When Indra learnt of this he invoked the demon Vighnasura, whose main occupation was to disturb Vedic rituals and *yagnas*. The Gods went to Ganesha, who fought and defeated Vighnasura. While accepting defeat, the demon requested Ganesha to pardon him and align his name with that of the God. The place where this battle was enacted is Ozar and the Lord is known as 'Vighneshwar Vinayaka' (the conqueror of Vighnasur).

Sri Girijatmaj of Lenyadri

Lenyadri connotes a cave and this temple is carved out of a mountain. One has to climb 307 steps. The temple has an impressive hall 54 x 51 feet, with not a single pillar supporting it. The idol is not properly carved as it is believed that Ganesha sits with his back to the entrance of the hall and faces the other side of the mountain. Efforts to dig on the other side and get the full image of the Lord have proved unsuccessful. Thus, one can see only the right half of the face of Ganesha. There are 18 other caves along with this, but they have been found inaccessible.

The legend avers that Goddess Parvati desired to have a son and undertook a rigorous penance for 12 years at this spot. Vinayaka was pleased and agreed to be her son. He took the form of her son and since he is the son of Girija, he is known as Girijatmaj—*atmaj* meaning son. Lord Ganesha spent 15 years here and destroyed the *asuras* who used to disturb the *yagnas* of *rishis*, who resided in the wild forests of this mountainous region.

Sri Varad Vinayak of Mahad

This temple is carved out of stone. There is a small pond behind the temple, and it is believed that the present idol was recovered from the pond sometime in 1690. The temple was constructed during the reign of the Marathas and renovated by the British rulers. In 1738, the saint Harihar Gosavi attained *samadhi* in this place.

To cut to the legend, the King of Vidarbha—Bhim was very brave, but unfortunately had no children. His prayers to Ganesha endowed him with a son named Rukmangad. Once Rukmangad went to the forest to hunt and was very tired and thirsty. He reached the *ashram* of Rishi Vaishnavi. The wife of the rishi, Mukunda saw the handsome

Prince and promptly became infatuated. The King turned down her request to fulfill her desire to marry him. Angry at being spurned, she cursed him to become a leper. Rukmangad performed penance for long years to free himself from the curse. Narada happened to meet him and advised him to bathe in the Kadamb Lake to restore normalcy. The King did so and was freed of leprosy. Indra who came to know of the infatuation of Mukunda, disguised himself as Rukmangad and had relations with her. This union led to the birth of a son named Gritsamada. This boy grew up to be a learned, brave and noble person, but some knowledgeable *rishis* belittled him on the grounds of his birth. Completely shattered, Gritsamada retreated to the forests. He performed severe *tapas* for years, stood on one leg and ate only dry leaves. He recited the famous Ganesha mantra *gananamtva ganapatim havamahe kavim kavinaam upamastra vasthamam*. Finally Ganesha gave him a boon which made him such a renowned *rishi* that his name came to be chanted at the start of Ganesha *mantra*. Since Lord Vinyaka gave the boon here, he is known as 'Varad Vinayaka'.

Sri Ballaleshwar of Pali

The idol here is 3 feet high. A special attraction is the big bell in the temple made of *panchadatu*—alloy of five elements. This bell was manufactured in Europe and brought to India and installed in the church of Vasai-sasti in Konkan. Chimaji Appa—a Maratha who had defeated the Portuguese brought this bell from the church and installed it in the temple.

Before one enters the main temple, one finds a Dhundi Vinayaka, which is said to be swayambhu. This Ganesha is typically worshipped first. The main idol wears a *dhothi* like a Brahmin, and this is the only Ganesha temple bearing the name of the worshipper. Let us turn to that story now.

A grocer named Kalyan had a son named Ballal, who was so fond of worshipping Ganesha that he took his friends to the forest as well. When other parents complained of the bad influence that Ballal had, his father became wild and went into the forest in search of his son.

He found him in deep contemplation and beat him mercilessly till he started bleeding. Kalyan tied Ballal to a tree and went home. He also smashed all *puja* materials and cast away the idol his son worshipped. The boy prayed to Ganesha who took the form of a Brahmin and restored Ballal to normalcy. Ballal recognised that the Brahmin was Ganesha and asked as a boon that the Lord stay permanently in the forest. The Brahmin disappeared and in his place, a black rock appeared with the form of Ganesha carved on it. The idol came to be known as Ballaleshwara and wears a *dhothi* like a Brahmin. The idol Kalyan had cast away is known as the Dhundi Vinayaka.

Sri Chintamani of Theur

This is a temple originally built by Gosavi Moraya and renovated by Madhavrao Peshwa. Here again, one finds bells brought from Portugal. On the ghats of the adjoining Mula Mutha river, the wife of Madhavrao Peshwa committed *sati*.

To recount the legend, Prince Gana, the son of King Abhijit was a very brave warrior. He went to the *ashram* of Kapila *rishi*, where he saw the diamond Chintamani—a magic diamond, which could bring forth anything the owner wanted. Gana asked the *rishi* to give it to him. When the latter refused, he snatched it from him. Kapila worshipped Ganesha, who was so pleased with his devotion that he got the diamond back for him after destroying Gana. By this time, Kapila had lost interest in Chintamani and did not take it back. He requested Ganesha to stay in its place. Ganesha remained there under a kadamba tree and took the name 'Chintamani Vinayaka'. The village is called Kadamb tirth.

Sri Mayureshwar of Morgaon

Mor in Marathi connotes peacock and the village of Morgaon not only had lots of peacocks, but its configuration resembled a peacock. The temple structure was built during the Mughal reign, though the idol is more ancient. A distinguishing feature of this temple is that a giant black Nandi is ensconced facing the idol of Ganesha. Nandi is the *vahana* of Shiva and is normally found facing a *shiva linga*. It is believed that the cart carrying a Nandi for a Shivalaya broke down just as it reached the Ganesha temple. It got stuck there and no efforts to take it out succeeded. The cart driver had a dream the next night that the Nandi wanted to remain there. So the Nandi continues to face Lord Ganesh.

The idol of Ganesha is in a sitting posture and has diamonds on its eyes. Due to constant application of *sindur*, the original shape is supposed to have been lost. The vermilion comes off once in a 100 years—last in 1882. Now for the legend—Chakrapani, a king had no son for years. He worshipped the Sun God and was blessed with a son named Sindhu. The son also worshipped the sun and was blessed with immortality. He conquered the world, as also Indra and Vishnu. Thereafter, he proceeded to conquer Kailas. All gods prayed to Ganesha to avert this. Ganesha took an *avatar* as the son of Parvati. He fought a great battle and defeated Sindhu or Kamalasur and killed him, cutting his body into three pieces. The head fell near Morgaon and the villagers constructed a temple here. Ganesha fought this battle on a peacock and he was known as Mayureshwar. This peacock was gifted by him to his brother Karthikeya.

Sri Siddhivinayak of Siddhatek

Siddhatek means a place where one gets *siddhi* or success. This is the only temple in our itinerary where Ganesha's trunk turns to the right. The present structure of the temple was built by the Peshwas, and Queen Ahilya Bai Holkar built the sanctum sanctorum. Maharishi Vyasa, Moraya Gosavi and Narayan Maharaj have prayed in this temple and obtained success. Even Lord Vishnu worshipped Ganesha here and obtained *siddhi*.

The legend has it that two demons Madhu and Kaitaba emerged from the wax in ears of Vishnu and created trouble for Brahma. Lord Vishnu—woken up from his cosmic slumber failed to defeat the two demons. He sought the advice of Shiva, who asked him to worship Ganesha. Vishnu undertook a penance and uttered for the first time the prayer, *Om Sri Ganeshaya Namaha*. Pleased by Vishnu's penance, Ganesha fought and destroyed the demons. The place where Vishnu was blessed by Ganesha is known as Siddhatek and Ganesha is known as Siddhivinayaka.

Shri Mahaganapati of Ranjangaon

The temple dates back to the 19th century and the sanctum sanctorum was constructed by Madhavrao Peshwa in 1768. It is believed that in the basement below the main idol, there is another idol of Ganesha with 10 trunks and 20 hands.

Gritsamada, a devotee of Ganesha, had a son who wanted to conquer all the three *lokas* as he grew up. Advised by his father, he prayed to Ganesha who blessed him with extraordinary powers and said that only Shiva can defeat him. He also gave him three cities made of steel, silver and gold. This Prince became an *asura* known as Tripurasura. He conquered all the three *lokas* and started humiliating all gods. Finally the Gods rushed to Shiva, who worshipped Ganesha and killed Tripurasura destroying the three cities. The place where Shiva worshipped Ganesha came to be known as Ranjangaon and the Ganesha as 'Mahaganapati'.

For those interested, there is an excellent book 'Ganesha' by Shakuntala Jagannathan and Nanditha Krishna, with splendid illustrations, both in colour and black and white.

The main Ganesha legends are sourced from the Shiva purana, Linga purana, Brahmavaivarta purana, Skanda purana, Varaha purana, Matsya purana and Padma purana. Two Upapuranas—the Ganesha purana and Mudgala purana also have stories of Ganesha.

Nainital

Nainital is a town in Uttarakhand and the head quarters of Nainital district in the Kumaon foothills of the outer Himalayas. Situated at an altitude of 1,938 m above sea level, Nainital is set in a valley containing a pear shaped lake, approximately 2 miles in circumference, and surrounded by mountains, of which the highest are Naina (2,615 m) on the north, Deopatha (2,438 m) on the west, and Ayarpatha (2,278 m) on the south. From the tops of the higher peaks, magnificent views can be obtained of the vast plain to the south, or the mass of the tangled ridges lying north, bounded by the great snowy range that forms the central axis of the Himalayas.

It is believed that Nainital figures in some ancient myths of India. In the Manas Khand of the Skanda Purana, Nainital lake is called Tri-Rishi-Sarovar, hinting at the story of three sages—Srti, Pulastya and Pulaha, who, upon finding no water in Nainital, dug a large hole at the location of the present day lake and filled it with water from the holy lake Manasarovar in Tibet. According to lore, a dip in Naini lake, 'the lesser Manasarovar,' earns merit equal to a dip in that great lake.

It is also believed that Naini lake is one of the 64 shakti peethas, or religious sites, where parts of the charred body of Sati (Parvati) fell on earth while being carried by Lord Shiva from the *kund* of the sacrifice arranged by Daksha. The spot where Sati's eyes (or *nain*) fell came to be called Nain-tal (or the lake of the eye). The Goddess Shakti is worshipped at the Naina Devi Temple on the north shore of the present day lake.

The town of Nainital was founded only in 1841, with the construction of the first European house by P. Barron, a sugar trader. Soon, the town became a health resort favoured both by British soldiers and by colonial officials and their families trying to escape the heat of the plains. Later, the town also became the summer residence of the Governor of United Provinces.

In September 1880, a landslide occurred at the north of the town, burying 151 people. The assembly rooms and the Naina Devi Temple were destroyed in the disaster. A recreation area known as 'The Flats' was later built on the site, and a new temple was also erected. In the latter half of the 19th century, a number of 'European' schools for boys and girls were founded in Nainital. During the Victorian and Edwardian eras, students in these schools consisted largely of children of British colonial officials or soldiers. In the 1920s and 1930s, the schools began to admit more Indian students. This trend continued until Independence by when the student bodies had become predominantly Indian, although in many cases greatly reduced in size.

By the 1880s, a mere 40 years after its founding, Nainital had become something of an exclusive English preserve, with the Indian presence in the town confined largely to a behind the scenes labour and service industry, or to the occasional prince. This state of affairs lasted for much of the Victorian Era. The first signs of change came early in the 20th century, when the bureaucrats and professionals began arriving as part of the annual migration of the state government of the United Provinces to Nainital every summer. From then on until 1947, the British presence in Nainital continued to decline and was gradually replaced by a burgeoning Indian presence.

Naina Devi Temple

The temple, destroyed by the landslide of 1880 and later rebuilt, is located on the northern shore of Naini lake. The presiding deity of the temple is Ma Naina Devi represented by two entraps or eyes. Flanking Naina Devi are deities of Ma Kali and Lord Ganesha.

The Governor's House was built in 1889 and designed in the Victorian Gothic domestic style by the architect F.W. Stevens (Stevens was architect of V.T. and Bombay Municipal Corporation buildings). Originally built as the summer residence of the Governor of the North West Province, it later became the summer residence for the Lieutenant Governor of the United Provinces. Currently, Raj Bhavan is the official guest house for the Governor of Uttarakhand. The complex consists of a two storied mansion with 113 rooms, a large garden, a swimming pool and a golf club.

Snow View (altitude 2,270 m) located atop the Sher-ka-danda Ridge is easily reachable by a cable car. On a clear day, it offers spectacular views of the snow bound high Himalayas, including Nandadevi, Trisul, and Nanda Kot.

Naina (also China, or Cheena) Peak is the highest peak in the town, with an altitude of 2,615 m and at a walking distance of 6 km from north end of the town (Mallital). From atop the peak, one can see not only a broad swath of the snow clad high Himalayas, but also obtain a panoramic view of Nainital town itself. The summit is an invigorating hike from Nainital town.

Gurney House—The former house of Jim Corbett is located on Ayarpatha hill. The house is now a museum of Corbett memorabilia.

Bhim Tal is a lake named after Bhima known for his prodigious strength. The lake, which is larger than the Naini lake, is approximately 22 km from Nainital at an altitude of 1,370 m. There is an island in the lake with a popular resort on it. There is also a 17th century temple complex—the Bhimeshwar, alongside a 40 feet high dam at one end of the lake. Naukuchia Tal (literally, nine cornered lake) is 26 km from Nainital and 4 km from Bhimtal at an altitude of 1,220 m. The lake is almost 1 km wide and approximately 40 m deep. It is the deepest of the lakes in the greater Nainital area. According to legend, if one takes in all nine corners in one glimpse, one can disappear in a cloud of smoke.

Hanuman Garhi (altitude 1,951 m)—The temple complex is about 3.5 km from the Tallital (south end) bus top. The presiding deity of the temple is Lord Hanuman, and he is depicted tearing open his chest to reveal Rama and Sita in his heart. Hanuman Garhi is also known for its spectacular views of the setting sun. While only seven of us saw the magnificent sunset, the majority stayed back in the hotel to watch India play miserable cricket!

Ranikhet is a hill station and cantonment town in Almora district at an altitude of 1,829 m and within sight of the western peaks of the Himalayas. Ranikhet, which means Queen's meadow in English, gets its name from a legend that a 12th century Indian Queen Rani Sukherdev visited the site and built herself a palace here, though no palace exists in this area. In 1869, the British established the head quarters of Kumaon regiment here. Ranikhet is a cantonment town and the home of the Kumaon Regimental Centre and maintained by the army.

Ranikhet offers a vast diversity of flora and fauna with dense forests of Pine and Deodar. One can see leopards in Ranikhet as well.

Jhula Devi Temple is a temple of Goddess Durga. It is an 8th century old temple, and it is believed that if a person asks for something he gets it and on fulfillment of his desire ties a bell in the temple. It is believed that a tiger visits the temple once a month and only the priest can see it.

Dronagiri is 52 km from Ranikhet where lies the 1100 century old Dronagiri temple. It is said that during the battle between Rama and Ravana, when Lakshman got hurt by the arrow of Meghanath, Hanuman went to obtain Sanjivani from Himalayas. On his way back a part of Sanjivani fell at the place called Dronagiri. Five km away from Dronagiri is the famous cave of Pandavkholi, where it is believed that Pandavas stayed during their exile.

Corbett National Park and Tiger Reserve lies 180 km northeast of New Delhi in the Nainital and Pauri Garhwal districts of Uttarakhand. Named after the celebrated hunter turned naturalist Jim Corbett who immortalised the area through his famous books, Corbett is India's first National Park and was established in 1936. It was earlier known as Hailey and Ramganga Park.

Encompassing 1,318 sq kms of foothills of the western Himalayas and the adjacent Terai region, Corbett Park contains a wide range of habitats numbering between 400 and 1,200. The thick Sal forests in the Bhabar zone and the *chaurs* (or open grass land) are intersected by river valleys and streams—tributaries of the Ramganga and Kosi rivers creating primeval forests, which are a hot spot of biodiversity.

While Corbett is justly famous for its healthy population of large mammals including the Indian Tiger and Asiatic Elephant, it is as famous for its birds with over 500 species recorded from the area. We undertook a safari at 5 am in an open Gypsy with a guide. We saw clusters of peacock, groups of spotted deer and monkeys, but of tigers—not one! It is wisely said that in forests 'guarantees are not given'. Even if you spend seven days and nights in a Machan in the reserve, a tiger may not present itself. *Kismet ka khel*!

Jim Corbett (1875-1955) was an Indian born hunter, conservationist and naturalist, famous for his writings on the hunting of man-eating tigers and leopards. Edward James 'Jim' Corbett was born at the town of Nainital in the Kumaon foothills of the Himalayas in 1875. Jim was the 8th child of Christopher and Mary Jane Corbett. Christopher Corbett was the postmaster of Nainital. Jim Corbett completed his matriculation exams in Nainital's Philanders Smith College. When Jim was 18, he joined the railways at Mokama Ghat in Bihar working as fuel inspector and assistant station master. He was a hunter and fishing enthusiast in early life, but took to big game photography later. As his admiration for the beautiful cats grew, he resolved never to shoot them unless they turned man-eaters or posed a threat to cattle. Between 1907 and 1938, Corbett tracked and put down at least a dozen man-eaters. It is estimated that the combined total of men, women and children that these 12 animals had killed (before Corbett sent them to the happy hunting grounds) was in excess of 1,500. His very first success was responsible for 436 documented deaths. He also shot the Panar Leopard, which allegedly killed 400 after being injured by a poacher and thus, being rendered unable to hunt his prey. Jim Corbett was tall (6'1'), brave and endowed with very keen senses. He would often stalk to within 20 feet or so of the man-eaters, and at great risk to himself to, as he put it, save at least one human life. He preferred to hunt alone when pursuing dangerous game, and on foot.

He was a pioneer conservationist and lectured at local schools and societies to stimulate awareness of the natural beauty surrounding local people and the need to conserve forests and their wildlife. He established India's first National Park, at first called the Hailey Park, named after Lord Malcolm Hailey, a former Governor of United Provinces, which was inaugurated in 1934 in the Kumaon Hills. He also had a deep affection for the people of the Kumaon Hills, and was loved by many of the region. He is considered by some in the Kumaon region as a *sadhu*.

After 1947, Corbett and his sister Maggie retired to Nyeri, Kenya, where he continued to write about declining numbers of jungle cats and other wildlife. Jim Corbett was at the Tree Tops hotel, a hut built on the branches of giant ficus tree. When Princess Elizabeth stayed there on February 5-6, 1952, at the time of the death of her father, King George VI, Corbett wrote in the hotel's visitors' register:

"For the first time in the history of the world a young girl climbed into a tree one day a Princess, and after having what she described as her most thrilling experience, she climbed down from the next day a Queen—God bless her."

Jim Corbett died of a heart attack a few days after he finished writing his sixth book—'Tree Tops', and was buried at St Peter's Anglican Church in Nyeri. The National Park he fought to establish in India was renamed in his honour two years later, and is now nearly twice its original size. It is a favourite place for visitors hoping to see a tiger. His accounts of hunting and killing man-eaters, which had killed almost 1,500 Indians, are related in his books: 'Man-Eaters of Kumaon', 'The Man-Eating Leopard of Rudraprayag' and the 'Temple Tiger and More Man-Eaters of Kumaon'. His 'Jungle Lore' is considered as his autobiography. He also wrote 'My India' about Indian rural life.

In 1968, one of the five remaining subspecies of tigers was named after him: Panthera Tigris Corbetti, more commonly called Corbett's Tiger.

Akshardham (Delhi)

Akshardham is a Hindu temple in Delhi inaugurated in November 2005 by the Indian President Abdul Kalam. The main building at the centre of the complex houses an 11 feet high, gilded image of Swaminarayan. The building itself is built of Rajasthani pink sandstone and Italian Carrara marble. At 141 feet high, its impressive presence is felt from far, and its carved details of flora, fauna, dancers, musicians and Gods covering its surfaces from top to bottom, leave most visitors in awe. Akshardham Delhi is the biggest hand carved structure in the world today.

The Yagnapurush Kund is India's largest step well. It features a very large series of steps down to a traditional *yagna kund*. At night, visitors take their places on the steps and watch an inspiring musical fountain and light show.

The *Bharat Upavan* or 'Garden of India' has lush manicured lawns, trees and shrubs, dotted with bronze sculptures of contributors to India's culture, including children of India and heroes of India. This ingenious sunken garden, shaped like a lotus when viewed from above features large stones engraved with quotes by world luminaries, ranging from Shakespeare, Vivekananda and Swaminarayan himself. Akshardham is the creation of Pramukh Swami Maharaj, the current spiritual leader of BAPS Swaminarayan Sanstha. Akshardham was created under his guidance after his *guru* Yogi Maharaj expressed a wish for the construction of the complex. He has created international cultural complexes like Swaminarayan Akshardham in Gandhinagar (India) and the Shri Swaminarayan Mandir in London, England (popularly known as the Neasden temple).

Swaminarayan Akshardham in New Delhi epitomises 10,000 years of Indian culture in all its breathtaking grandeur, beauty, wisdom and bliss. It brilliantly showcases the essence of India's ancient architecture, traditions and timeless spiritual messages. The Akshardham experience is an enlightening journey through India's glorious art, values and contributions for the progress, happiness and harmony of mankind. The grand, ancient-styled Swaminarayan Akshardham complex was built in only five years through the colossal devotional efforts of 11,000 artisans and BAPS volunteers.

Akshardham means the eternal divine abode of the supreme God, the abode of eternal values and virtues of *akshar* as defined in the Vedas and Upanishads, where divine *bhakti*, purity and peace forever pervades.

Harihareshwar-Srivardhan-Diveagar-Murud Janjira

After offering prayers to my father-in-law on the occasion of his first death anniversary in Pune, we went on a two day trip to lovely Konkan. We included three of his daughters, sons-in-law and one close relative.

We hired a Qualis and the seven of us had quite a comfortable ride, except where the roads were bumpy. The weather was salubrious, the wind wafting from the sea made it quite pleasant.

Our first halt was Harihareshwar and our first item on the menu was a sumptuous lunch at a bungalow converted into a hotel. Food was hot and tasty—though some in our team suffered from a morbid fear of *lassoon* (garlic). They dreaded this aphrodisiac as if it were some kind of vicious poison! The high-water mark of the lunch was piping hot large-sized *modaks* made of coconut shreds and garnished with *gur* and *ghee*. Pure delight!

Harihareshwar is Maharashtra's Murdeshwar, a sunny temple town by a sylvan, palm-lined beach. The town is called Dakshina Kashi—in fact, people throng this sleepy town for paying respects to departed parents. There is the famous Kalabhairava temple that has as much a sense of timelessness to it as the waves lapping against the seashore. The temple is believed to have been established by Sage Agasthya—he is called Agastyhi here. Evidence suggests that it was constructed during the reign of Shivaji and there are records of his visit to this temple in 1774. The temple was rebuilt by the first Peshwa—Balaji Viswanath.

At the rear of the temple are steps leading to the top of the hill and confronted by a huge boulder split into half. According to legend, the Pandavas, while in exile had visited Harihareshwar. Finding their path blocked by a boulder, Bhima wielded his fist and smashed the rock into two. At the bottom, towards the right, is a cleft in another rock from which issues forth sweet, potable water. Down there, beside a huge boulder is the footprint of Bhima carved in rock. But it was under water and we could not see it. This spot is called Pandav Tirth.

This narrow cleft is 3 feet wide between rocks and steps take you down to the sea. At the bottom of this cleft, there is a niche and when the waters recede, a Ganesh idol can be seen. The place is called Ganesh Gully. All of us saw the Ganesha at a distance of 10 feet.

The Harihareshwar beach is 1 ½ kms long and split into two parts—north and south—by the Kalabhairav Temple. The sand is not as white as in other beaches.

Harihareshwar is the abode of God. Sage Vasishta had declared this to be the town from where one can attain salvation and be freed of the cycle of birth and death. So people come here for performing rituals for their dead relations. Once upon a time, two demons were harassing the local Konkani people. Lord Harihar came to their rescue and he and Mother Goddess brought the two demons back to the righteous path. A *yagna* was planned with Goddess Savithri to perform the ceremonies, but she forgot about it and failed to turn up. Goddess Gayathri stood in for her. Savithri became angry and converted Gayathri into a river and all those who attended the *yagna* were turned into water. This injustice made Vishnu turn Savithri into a river and bring back to life all the people made into water. The river flows into the Arabian Sea between Harihareshwar and Bagmandala. A few miles from here is Vellas—the village where the Peshwa Nana Phadnavis was born.

The next place on our itinerary was Srivardhan—the place of A.R. Antulay, which is more famous for its beaches, temples, historic monuments. The virgin sands at Kondivili beach will take your breath away. They shine like diamonds and are brown-black in colour. Srivardhan is the birthplace of Balaji Vishwanath, the founder of the Peshwa dynasty, who took power during the reign of Shivaji's grandson, Shahu Maharaj. The presiding deity here is Somaji Devi. People bitten by snakes are brought here and placed on a solid boulder—curved in shape. No medicines are used, but the wounds are cauterised by hot coals. After this the *pundits* use cool peacock feathers. The patients are cured.

There is a 200-300 year old Shankar temple. The house where Baji Rao I was born is preserved and there is a statue of the Peshwa. This Peshwa succeeded in raising the Maratha banner over the distant Mughal kingdom of Malwa, and reached as far as the Chambal. He plundered the Mughal province of Avadh and his men set fire to the capital Delhi. He was only 40 years when he died prematurely.

Our last trip was to Murud Janjira—a 12th century fort built by the *siddis* (Muslims from Africa). We had to take a motor launch from Srivardhan to Dighi. From there to the fort we had to go in a boat— with sails—rowed by three persons. Quite thrilling it was. Dighi beach is of course, where RDX was landed for the Bombay March 12, 1993 blasts.

Janjira Fort was built in 1174—it took 22 years to build on an area of 22 acres and it has 22 outposts from where cannons were fired. The *siddis* were fierce warriors, who hailed from Abyssinia. The fort is believed to be under the protection of the Panch Peer Panjatan Shah Baba, whose tomb greets visitors on entry. Rising 90 feet above the sea with a 20 feet strong foundation, nobody could conquer the *siddis*. It is called *ajinkya*—unconquerable. As the story goes Sambhaji planted a mango seed the year he arrived. The tree grew and Sambhaji partook of its fruits, but the fort never fell. Begum Zubeida had her 'Sheesh Mahal' in this fort. There is a fresh water pond and 550 families stayed in the fort. It had a subterranean tunnel leading to the village half a mile away. Since the landing of RDX nearby, this fort is under the supervision of Indian Navy and no one is allowed to enter the fort. The last of the *siddis* Ahmed Shah Siddi has a palace called Ahmedganj Palace, which is noted for its opulence.

Sambhaji built a fort known as Padmadurg Fort—named after his wife. It is called the Kasa Fort.

Diveagar is famous for its solid Ganesha statue in gold, emerald and rubies. This idol was found in a box full of diamonds dug up by a lady 1000 years ago from a field. It is 11 to 12 kgs of pure gold called the 'Sone-ki-Ganapati'.

Essays

28 Am I Successful as a Senior Citizen?

The oldest of all riddles is 'the riddle of the sphinx'. The sphinx, a monster with a human head and the body of a beast, sat on a high rock by the roadside near the city of Thebes, in Egypt. To every passerby, she asked:

"What is it that has but one voice, and goes on four feet, then on two, and lastly on three?"

Those who could not answer were strangled and thrown from a height. Only one man, the Greek Oedipus could answer and he said:

"Man—because he crawls on all fours as an infant, then walks on two feet and in old age uses a staff or a cane."

Let us take the last part of Oedipus's answers. Is a senior citizen one who uses a staff or cane? Answering this riddle in modern times does call for some background.

Life expectancy these days is 75 years with the result that if one retires at 58 or 60, half the working life is left after retirement. Family structure has vastly changed and today's family unit consists of the father, the mother and two or less children. By the time one retires, the daughter is married and has gone away. Nowadays sons also go away after marriage, leaving the mother and father to fend for each other! Earlier one could claim 'roots'; go to native places and ancestral homes. Today, people struggle to decide where to settle down.

In view of the three vital clues given above, senior citizens face genuine problems. They have usually worked for 30 years or more and are at the peak of their career, status, prestige and monetary position. Suddenly, one evening all these entirely grind to a halt. No longer are you 'Numero Uno'. A simple instance of your shrinking importance is that while in service you get hundreds of greeting cards, scores of diaries and sundry gifts—all these become a trickle after retirement!

Another factor is that while in service you have had no time for anything, now you have 24 hours and nothing to do. So it is imperative that unless you want slow death by inanition, you must cultivate some good habits, acquire some new interests, indulge in hobbies and keep yourself occupied all the 24 hours.

With this scarcely pleasant scenario, I shall recount how successful I am as a senior citizen. I am a postgraduate in Economics from the University of Bombay. After retirement, at the age of 60, I joined the Department of Sanskrit at the University of Bombay and acquired a Certificate and Diploma in Sanskrit as also postgraduate Diploma in Comparative Mythology. I competed on equal terms with students of the age of my daughters and won prizes for an essay on Kalidasa and a recitation from 'Raghuvamsam'.

I have been for several years, a member of the Book Selection Committee of the prestigious Asiatic Library. I am also adviser for the last three years of the S.V. Phatak Memorial Library at Vile Parle. This involves visiting bookstalls and has resulted in making available quality books leading to improved standards of the readers.

I am a keen and careful reader of books and have correspondences with several great writers—my bunch of letters include those from Khushwant Singh, R.K. Laxman, Natwar Singh, Paul Gallico, Jeffrey Archer, Sucheta Dalal, I.G. Patel, M. Narasimham and the respected C. Rajagopalachari and Dr S. Radhakrishnan.

Music and movies are a passion with me, and I am member of several cultural organisations such as Shanmukhananda Sabha and Prabhat Chitra Mandal. I regularly attend programmes and took part in a two day seminar on Music Therapy about which I wrote an article in a website. Recently I ran a series of six articles in this site on 'Matunga Musings', which allowed senior citizens to indulge in nostalgia and offered enlightenment to junior citizens. I have written on foreign Ramayanas, Nadaswaram—a wind instrument and other topics. A successful senior citizen should impart the benefit of his knowledge and experience to the next generation and I do make a contribution here.

Reviewing books is one of my favourite pastimes. I have reviewed books on banking and management in the bulletins of the Indian Banks Association as also in the quarterly Reserve Bank of India house journal *Without Reserve*. All these articles are read by a large number of young readers and I have, as a senior citizen, established a direct link with the leaders of tomorrow.

For students going abroad for advanced studies, a vital document is the 'SOP'—the Statement of Purpose. It states what the student's achievements and aims are as well as the steps he will take to reach his goal. It is a statement of about four paragraphs, which presents all details succinctly. I have become a bit of regular SOP guide and those whom I have helped, have got admission and are presently undertaking advanced studies in US, UK, etc. Some students were expressly commended for their crisp SOP.

If charity begins at home, I begin my activity chart from the society I reside in. I have made myself responsible for keeping our environment scrupulously clean, engaging myself in collecting funds and ensuring that cleanliness is observed in fact and spirit. I monitor daily the activity of the staff allotted this work.

We have a Senior Citizens Club, which is 12 years young. I am an active member, and club activities include arranging periodical medical camps, excursions to places of interest. We also hold regular meetings, the latest—presenting a music programme with the doyen of journalists, Shri M.V. Kamath as the Chief Guest.

Since I have served for four decades in the country's Central bank, I am in a position to lecture to staff of banks on banking, management, motivation and the art of living. I have engaged sessions of students of standards nine and ten of the schools in our area on topics like 'Humour and the English language'. Spontaneous and lively reaction of children is an elixir to me. Students explode with healthy laughter and find the sessions lively and useful.

Today's world is a 'quizzical' world and I have acquired much expertise in conducting quiz programmes. This, I have done in Parle, enabling students to enlarge their knowledge and improve their responses. Subjects covered included politics, government, personalities, history, science, sports, the fine arts and a cliff hanging rapid fire round.

BBC's Mastermind India is a quiz programme to conjure with. In the preliminary written test, out of 2,000 candidates only 64 were declared successful and I was one of the 64 at 64 years. On the day of the quiz, I stood second, being defeated by a youth of my daughter's age. The quiz master, Siddharth Basu was so much impressed with the zest of a senior citizen that he asked me to contribute questions to the popular show by Amitabh Bachchan Kaun Banega Crorepati. I did.

All work and no play makes Jack a dull boy. A senior citizen with so many assignments does require a diversion. This is provided by my two grandchildren—a granddaughter who is the 'apple' of my eye and a grandson who is the 'appoos' of my eye. Hours fly in their company, in their childish pranks, in their intelligent questions and their honest response to all queries and all situations. To have grandchildren sitting on one's lap listening to stories is the true definition of joy.

Every evening I spend two hours with a band of young men and women as part of an international quizzing agency. We devise questions and answers and put them in different formats. This work, where my rich experience and familiarity with quizzing is of great assistance, offers an intellectual challenge.

Baba Amte said, "Don't add years to your life; add life to your years." As a senior citizen, I find this advice wholesome and I make every effort to live up to it. Senior citizenship is not resting on one's oars, recalling the past or doling out advice gratuitously. Life is a challenge and I have not allowed 66 years to dim my enthusiasm.

One has to accept the challenge and take the bull by its horns. A variety of interests and a determined effort to pursue one's aims have stood me in good stead for becoming a successful senior citizen. Jawaharlal Nehru declared, "Success comes to those who dare and do. It seldom goes to the meek." This is applicable as much to the young and aspiring as to senior citizens, who have only a few years to spend in this wonderful world. They can, by will and efforts, make these years rich and become successful senior citizens.

29 Confusion about *Avataras*

The 10 *avataras* of Vishnu are as given below.

1. Matsya
2. Kurma
3. Varaha
4. Narasimha
5. Vamana
6. Parasurama
7. Rama
8. Krishna
9. Buddha
10. Kalki

It is axiomatic that one *avatara* is succeeded by another. Lord Krishna himself declared in the Gita, *Sambahavami yuge yuge.*

The fifth *avatara* is that of Vamana, who is Vishnu in dwarf form. He took three steps, covering the heavens in one step and the earth in the second step. With his third step, he pushed King Bali or Mahabali into *patala*. The legend goes that Mahabali was the king in Kerala and appears every year during Onam to meet his happy subjects, who cherish his memory.

The legend also goes that Kerala was formed by Parashurama—the sixth *avatara*—who threw his axe into the sea and carved out a piece of land for Brahmins to live in peace. The Brahmins were earlier oppressed by the Kshatriyas, and Parasurama was born to decimate them.

So, how can Vamana, the fifth *avatara* be co-terminus with the next -sixth *avatara*-Parasurama? The first confusion!

Now here is the second confusion:

In the Ramayana, Parasurama, a follower of Lord Shiva felt aggrieved by Rama's breaking the bow of Shiva and challenged Rama to a duel—a trial of strength. This ended in his defeat and in some way led to his being 'excluded from a seat in the celestial world'.

How can Parasurama—the sixth *avatara*—coexist with the next i.e. the seventh *avatara*, Rama?

Here is another related confusion:

Once, the ever angry Durvasa sage was pleased to give a fragrant garland to Indra, who promptly put it on his elephant Airavatha. The powerful smell of the garland attracted thousands of bees and distracted the tusker. Airavatha tore the garland and trampled on it. The sage was furious and cursed that Indra and all the *Devas* be afflicted with Jara and Nara. The only cure for the curse was to be found by churning the sea of milk. This churning led to nectar or *amritha*, which helped remove the affliction. The legend also states that many items emerged out of this *amritha manthan*, including the elephant Airavatha.

How does one explain this, if Airavatha is the cause of it all?

30 Religion in Today's World

When the Paramacharya of Kanchi Kamakoti Peetam attained salvation by renouncing his mortal frame, one of the important visitors to the mutt was the Ex-Justice Ismail. This Muslim *savant* is an authority on Hindu scriptures, Kamba Ramayanam and other Tamil classics, and used to be called often for discussions by the Paramacharya. Justice Ismail recalled how he had once requested the Sankaracharya to offer his advice and the latter told him, "You are a Muslim. Say your prayers five times a day as laid down in Islam. Be a good man."

Can we fail to perceive in this stimulating conversation the greatness of thoughts of two sublime minds? No proselytisation. No lecturing. No posturing. Only be true to your religion. Be good.

One of the greatest scientists of all times, Albert Einstein wrote, "The cosmic religious experience is the strongest and noblest mainspring of scientific research. My religion consists of a humble admiration of the illimitable superior spirit, who reveals himself in the slight details we are able to perceive with our frail and feeble minds. That deeply emotional conviction of the presence of a superior power, which is revealed in the incomprehensible universe, forms my idea of God."

The Bhagavad Gita, which is the quintessence of the thoughts of our ancient *munis*, contains a magnificent outpouring of noble poetry. All life is an encounter and the supreme encounter is that of man with God. Arjuna sees God as the entire universe. He is blinded by the brilliance, the veil is then torn and Krishna-Arjuna *samvadha* is enacted. It may be readily conceded that not all of us can scale the heights of Arjuna nor comprehend the effulgence of a meeting with the Almighty. In our own humble way, we can adopt religion as a way of life.

It is of no use to practice extreme penance to acquire esoteric knowledge. The parable of Ramakrishna is worth recounting. A certain saint approached him after a tough penance of seven years. Asked Ramakrishna, "And, what did you learn?" The saint replied, "I can walk over this river from our bank to the opposite bank." Ramakrishna laughed and said, "Our boatman will take you across for one pie."

We can adopt religion as a way of life and perform the duties allotted to us with sincerity and devotion, without a trace of selfishness. Doing one's duty is the highest form of religion.

Karl Marx declared, "Religion is the opium of the people." What he decried was the gross misuse of religion by the priestly class, who amassed wealth and power and used this tyrannically to oppress the backward and poor people.

Let's recall the rightly famous Chicago address of Swami Vivekananda at the World's Parliament of Religions. One paragraph is worth quoting again and again.

"I am proud to belong to a religion which has taught the world both tolerance and universal acceptance. We believe not only in universal toleration, but we accept all religions as true. I am proud to belong to a nation which has sheltered the persecuted and the refugees of all religions and all nations of the earth...."

I will quote from a hymn, which is repeated every day by millions......

"As the different streams having their sources in different places all mingle their water in the sea, O Lord, the different paths which men take through different tendencies, various though they appear, crooked or straight, all lead to thee."

From Vivekananda, we learn humility. When he visited Oxford, he called on Prof Max Muller, the great Indologist, than whom no one has done more for spreading knowledge of the 'Sacred Books of the East'. As soon as he saw the Muller couple, he prostrated at their feet. The old scholar picked him up with some surprise. Tears were flowing from the Swamiji's eyes. He told Muller, "To me, you are Vasishta and Arundhati." Such humility from a great saint should teach us all to be humble and not proud.

Let religion bring us all together. Let it unify. Let it strengthen and let it lead us to a better life and salvation.

ESSAYS »

31 The Quest for 'Vatapi Ganapati'

The great Indian trinity of South Indian classical music comprised of Tyagaraja (1767-1847), Muthuswami Dikshitar (1775-1835) and Shyama Shastri (1763-1827). It is a strange coincidence that all were born in Tiruvaraur and lived in adjoining streets. While there are records that Dikshitar frequently visited Shyama Shastri and compared notes on the music of their times, it is not known whether he met Tyagaraja.

Dikshitar was born in 1775 and was the youngest of the trio. While he lived only for 60 years and Shastri for 64 years, Tyagaraja was 80 when he departed. Together, the period in which they composed Carnatic music is rightly called the Periclean age, and during these 80 years, Europe too had its golden age with Mozart, Beethoven, Schubert and Weber pouring out their best.

Dikshitar's father was Ramaswami Dikshitar—an excellent *veena* player and a talented composer of Kritis, Varnams and Ragamalikas. His son overshadowed him. Muthuswami Dikshitar accompanied a Saint Chidambaranatha Yogi to Varanasi and spent five years studying philosophy. It is also likely that he went with his *guru* to Badrinath, Kathmandu and other North Indian shrines. On return to the South, he proceeded to Tiruttani and worshipped Lord Subrahmanya. Tradition has it that Dikshitar was in meditation and Lord Kumara came as an old man and put sugar candy in his mouth. He burst into song and rendered his first *kriti Sri Nathadi Guruguho* in the *raga mayamalavagaula*. He fitted in his compositions the name of the *raga* and his *mudra-guruguha*.

Dikshitar has to his credit 500 compositions. He composed a complete series of songs to illustrate the 72 *mela karta* scheme of Asampurna Mela Paddhati. He incorporated descriptions of temples, deities, goddesses, sacred tanks, trees, local customs and even beauties of architecture.

A matter for some surprise is that Dikshitar composed Sanskrit devotional texts for tunes of the English band of Chinnayya Mudaliar—in all 37 Nottusvaras, which included the British national anthem!

"If humility is the hallmark of Tyagaraja, piety the password of Shyama Shastri, then Dikshitar's works are like jewels made of words that are gems, so carefully entwined with pure traditional music", thus a perceptive critic summed up the Trinity.

Let us now turn to Dikshitar's composition *Vatapi Ganapatim Bhaje*. The story goes that the song is based on a statue of Lord Ganesha. Carnatic music concerts used to start with this *kriti*, thanks to the efforts and example of Vidwan Maha Vaidyanatha Iyer. The song is in melodious Hamsadvani and artistically captures the playful nature of Ganesha. Now, the question is where is this statue?

Kalki in his great historical novel 'Sivakamiyin Sabatham' presented one version.

Vatapi—a corruption of Badami is located in Bijapur. After the Pallavas (under the rule of Narasimha Varman (630-638 AD) conquered Badami, they brought an image of Ganapati to Tanjore and installed it in the Ganapatisvara temple of Tiruccengattangudi. This was the home of the Pallava General Paranjyoti, who changed his name to Ciruttonda and became a Shaivaite saint. However, oral traditions doubt this and believe that the Ganapati is installed in a secondary shrine.

At a later date, the idol served as an inspiration for another Ganapati in the Tiruvarur temple. This is the statue that Dikshitar made immortal with his mellifluous song, full of praise of Ganesha. A sketch of the Tiruvarur idol appeared in the issue of Kalki dated 23 June 1946, which also included an article by Kalki on 'Vatapi Ganapati'.

The quest for the original Vatapi Ganapati is still on.

32 My Grand 'G . . . . .'

In a jiffy he will shed all his clothes and present his *nanga darshan* in his tight shorts. As he is quite well built; he looks like a minor version of a Sumo wrestler. Don't misconstrue my account of his stripping as an escapade of a sex-maniac! Far from it. It is the transformation of my innocent grandson, who has walked all the way from school to Crystal Enclave in the torrid Mumbai sun, carrying on his back, a hefty school bag making him into a 'beast of burden'. No sooner he enters the house than he strips—casting away the smelly, sweat-drenched uniform.

A bit more about his school life. His uniform is an olive pant and yellow shirt with an olive tie. As we have an L-shaped balcony facing the main road, we have a grand view of the procession of students going up and down the road. From 6 am to 5 pm we see 100s of students in uniforms of varied hue running to schools in both the directions. As school closing time approaches, Ashish's grandmother ensconces herself in the balcony looking out for him. "Ha! Here he is!" she will exclaim sighting him from a distance. But it turns out to be another boy. So many look alikes. She will start the search again. Finally at 1 pm he arrives and quietly declares, "Patti, I forgot my umbrella." The things he has lost are pencil, ball-pen, textbook, notebook, eraser, water bottle and handkerchief. "Does not Priya (mother) fire you for losing things?" "No", he declares with a smile!! "Ever since she lost her laptop in an auto!" the clincher was, "To reach her level of loss I can lose items for a couple of years!"

His next activity after undressing is to switch on the TV and watch two serials—Shin Chan and Doraemon with utmost dedication and devotion for an hour. Meanwhile, Grandma has prepared his lunch and spread it on a large plate—small mounds of rice and *sambhar* with *karuvadam* (homemade fried delicacy). He will take mound by mound, transfer it to his mouth—chew and ingest, scarcely aware of what he is consuming! He will explode into loud laughter at intervals at the inane jokes of the programme.

More on this TV addict. At the precise moment when I received an award from BBC Mastermind for standing second in the grilling quiz competition conducted by Siddharth Basu, my first daughter Priya gave birth to her second child, a son she named Ashish. I do not know the connection between these two items, but undeniable is the fact that Ashish has grown into a great questioner—a seeker of knowledge. He asked Priya, "You know I am your son. But how do I know?" She explained, "The way you walk, the way you lisp, the shape of your ears, your gait—all resemble mine." Declared he, "Not enough." So she told him of DNA, Watson, Crick etc. He accepted. Going to the adjoining garden for a walk—he was five then—he rushed to an enormously pregnant lady, "Auntie, are there two inside?" You can imagine that lady's reaction and Priya's mortification!

One day I got an SOS call from Ashish, "Tatha, I want your help. And just now. Meri izzat ka baat hai." "Of course, I will help", I assured him. He demanded a story on 'Arrogance of Arjuna and Hanuman'. I told him an impressive story, which he absorbed fully and next morning recounted in his class to the total approval of his teacher and applause of his friends. If you do not know the story, I will gladly tell you.

Next day he spilled the beans. The teacher had asked in the class, "Can anyone tell a story tomorrow on 'Arrogance of Arjuna and Hanuman'?" Ashish promptly raised his hand. After their class was over, his friends asked him, "How can you be so confident?" This is what he told his friends, "Hamara ghar mey ek budda hai. Kuch kaam nai kartha hai. Padtha hai padtha hai. Magar achcha kahani dega." Translated into English-

"In our house there is an old man. He does no work except reading and reading. But he will give a nice story."

Between Ashish and his elder sister Ashwini, there is no love lost nor gained. They fight for chairs, ball-pens, *chappathis*, fruits, chocolates, place in their car, place in autos. But they love each other intensely. On one occasion when Ashish was hospitalised, Ashwini was brought in. She saw her brother in a bed immobile and his eyes closed. As she watched, tears gushed from her eyes. No amount of words could describe the pain she felt for her fond brother.

Ashish and Ashwini are submerged by the love of their paternal grandparents and with our shifting from Vile Parle to Kalina, close to their house; they will soon be showered with the love of maternal grandparents as well. If this is good or not I know not.

An important question.

What is common to Barack Obama, Leonardo da Vinci, Lewis Carroll, Amitabh Bachchan and Ashish Gopal?

All are left-handed!

33 Birth of Two 'P's

The stork has visited 102, Crystal Enclave. Two new items are bursting with élan and beauty, making life more meaningful and adding charm to the evening of our lives.

To begin at the beginning, our new house has two balconies christened 'Flowerbed Balconies' and a better choice for name cannot be thought of. One balcony is L-shaped—in all 16 feet long and 2 feet wide; the other is 6 feet by 2 feet. If nature abhors a vacuum, so does my wife, Lakshmy.

Thus, both the balconies are chockfull of pots with assorted plants. Much care and devotion is provided by this lady and within three months, we have had a mini garden of plants. As we moved in on January 26th, we had tremendous heat from a bountiful sun and this divine grace from the Sun God was fully utilised by my wife. Twice she brought copious quantities of fresh cow dung—availability guaranteed by nearby temples with cows and *gai-walis*. The whole house smelt of dung and urine, but this lady was supremely happy watching the solidification of dung with bouncing joy. When the liquid was transformed into solid, she cut it into small cakes and all the pots had their fill. Earlier they became holy by consuming *gomutra*. I had brought this hidden in thick bags so that it could not be seen.

The nature poet Wordsworth declared "My heart leaps up when I behold a rainbow." I am certain it scarcely leaped as high as my wife's heart leaped up when she beheld the first 'earthworm' of the new rainy season. No sooner the first of the new monsoon showers kissed the parched earth than she would run down to the passage of our building scouting for earthworms. She would return disappointed when none had emerged. One rainy day she returned as happy as a child, which has got a Cadbury chocolate. She said, "It is my lucky day. I have caught a dozen earthworms." And these slimy creatures, quaintly called *nakkapoochies* she diligently deposited in her pots as if she was placing roses at the feet of Guruvayoorappan. Prayers and efforts seldom fail. Lo and behold! This vermiculture venture had a miraculous effect on the plants and they grew merrily.

Light green turned into dark green; a few days later we had creepers climbing over our conveniently arranged parallel grills. In less than a month, we had a dozen tiny yellow flowers. Lakshmy would check each and every flower. A few fell off—with some tears from her too—but fresh ones would bloom. My wife was not exactly happy. "A summom bonum, devoutly to be wished for", as Hamlet put it, was not materialising. You could detect a certain wryness in her visage, but two days ago as I was sleeping at 11 am (I sleep anytime I like!), she poked into my ribcage. She was bursting with joy and declared, "I am very happy. I have two parikkais in my flowerbed garden." I was duly led to the balcony and she pointed out two tiny 'three inches growth' with the flowers at the end.

That, dear friends, is the story of the birth of two P's in Crystal Enclave. P.P. stands for *parikkai* and *parikkai*. Bitter gourd or *karela* for those who are unfamiliar with *parikkai*. As days advanced, she would ensconce herself before the tiny *parikkais*, register their progress. The two maiden *parikkais* have now grown—one almost full-grown. We have now three more green siblings.

My wife has what is called 'green hands'; whatever she plants grows in abundance. We were allotted a new bungalow by Reserve Bank of India (RBI) in Trivandrum. On day one it was barren, no greenery. Not one leaf, not one flower, not a vegetable, no fruit at all. She planted and grew papayas, tomatoes, tondlis, plantain, etc. Most amazing was curry leaves or *karuveppila, kadipatha*, which grew from 2 feet to 60 feet. You had to climb the tree to clutch at the wonderfully smelling leaves. We had a neem tree, which also grew to great height. One wall fully covered by *madrasi pan* or *vethilai*. In my Issue Department—I was Currency Officer—we had 20 officers who hailed from Chennai and were inveterate *pan* chewers. I would invite them regularly to my house and pluck *vethilai* to their hearts' content (Malli, are you hearing?). Of flowers, we had a bewildering variety. There was a bower of white *mullai* flowers. There were flowers of other hues as well.

To come to the present, now she looks happily at the new born *karelas* with as much love and affection as her own two P's—Priya and Pushpa! Now P and P stand for *parikkai* and *parikkai*. To end on a sweet note, when our grandson Ashish, who comes everyday for lunch with us surveyed our garden and declared, "Patti, my Kalina tatha likes karela very much. Will you give him the first two karelas?" "Of course", she said tears welling in her eyes for the grandson's care and affection for his 80 year old paternal grandfather. I doubt if at that moment someone told her that she had won Padma Shri she would not have been as happy as when acceding to her grandson's request.

34 My Dear 'Veda'

Of course, you have seen a 'rocking horse'. But have you seen a 'rocking bicycle'? No! I am not surprised—since I saw it myself for the first time in 75 years in my younger daughter Pushpa's house. This is a plastic bicycle, which has two wheels, pedals, huge handles at a height and the whole thing fixed to a semicircle base on which the child is supposed to rock. But this is precisely not what Veda is doing! She stands up on the seat and bends down and clutches the handles with her two arms. Sometimes she lets go one hand or the other—even shockingly enough, both the hands. When I saw this, I nearly had a heart attack. From her standing spot, the child could fall full one foot on the floor, or her face, nose and eyes could hit the handles. None of these fears appear to be known to the child—since she is all of 18 months and my latest granddaughter. I hide the rocking cycle, but she cajoled her mother and had it restored and started her acrobatics.

The other day Veda wanted to get something from a 110 years old table, I bequeathed to Pushpa. Veda could not reach it. So she dragged a small plastic box, brought it near the table, turned it over and kept one leg on it and was about to keep the other leg—there was space for half a leg only, when I got my second attack—you know which type. I rushed, secured her object of desire and gave it to her. She was all smiles.

Now about this bundle of mischief! She is very fair, supple with a rich crop of soft silken hair, which is flattened on her head. She is always enveloped in smiles and the occasions she cries in a day are one or two. She loves idlis and makes constant demand to her grandma—"Patti, idli, idli". The grandma has to run after her to make her eat two idlis. She drinks milk from a bottle, but never more than half. She is a great fan of Barney—that colourful cartoon character whose CD Veda will see for full hour sitting on my lap or that of the grandma. She will clap when the characters clap or dance in unison with them.

She sleeps during daytime for two hours, but rest of the time she is busy with her toys, kids' books and other playthings. Since my daughter has to attend to medical calls from USA, she locks herself in a room with a computer. Veda will say "Amma—office", but keep awake till Pushpa emerges at 11 pm. Here is where Barney acts as the saviour.

Veda is flourishing under the generous umbrella of her paternal grandmother Radha Mami—presently in New Jersey with her daughter and grandson Siddharth. Radha Mami and Veda miss each other so much that this lady will call every day and she will talk to her through the PC—both can see each other on the PC screen—with the help of web cameras. As evening advances, Veda will ask for Siddharth and Patti—and Hey! Presto!! They too feel the need to communicate and will call Pushpa. Dialogue continues for at least an hour—on food, dress, Siddharth's school, Veda's pranks of the day! Distance is demolished by the electronic waves.

Veda's vocabulary is growing daily! When she says 'Come' it means it is time for me to take her out! Come means go!! *Ukku* is the word for chikku. Where has Appa gone? 'Pain' she will tell you loudly and clearly...He has gone to Spain. Her favourite words are 'I loub you!!' For I love you! Every morning I put her in a pram, neatly bathed and dressed with a *pottu* of *vibhuthi* on her forehead. She will smile at all office-goers, school kids and say 'I loub you!' No wonder she is very popular. All wait and watch for her. And her confession of love.

We spent nine days—in the absence of her father who had to go to Spain and it was for us pure nectar. No tantrums, oozing with affection and spreading joy in the world with her smiles. One smile from Veda can light up this dark world.

35 All Done

Three months ago we paid a visit to Pune for three days to rejoice in the company of Veda. All of you have read 'My dear Veda'. This time we are spending three weeks to absorb this ambrosia aka Veda.

In this interval of three months, Veda has increased her vocabulary by leaps and bounds. She can sing 'Baa! Baa! Black Sheep!', count from 1 to 10, croon 'One, Two, Buckle My Shoe', call out for me 'Tatha' and Lakshmy as 'Patti'. But the most significant and paramount two words she has mastered are 'All done' delivered with the impact of bullets from an AK 47—noted for both power and speed. The two words mean an end of whatever activity she is undertaking presently. When Pushpa is feeding her with rice and curd, halfway through, she spits out the words 'All done' and that means—quite firmly—thus far and no further. *Na atra samsayaha.*

She acquired this phraseology from diligently watching a cartoon character Barney. When Veda shouts loudly, Barney that epic hero has to appear on the laptop screen. Or else there is hell to pay! Quite recently one more delightful character has swum into her ken -to wit, Elmo.

It is not as if only foreign characters have captured her attention. Her grandma—presently in New Jersey with her grandson—has made her familiar with a CD of lovely songs in Tamil with more lovely images—bears, squirrels, thirsty crow and events in our daily life. There is a dainty song, 'Dosai amma dosai' on the number of *dosais* to be eaten by each member of the family.

There is one trick I am quite adept at. I extend my right arm, make the child stand on my palm and lift him or her up. Suddenly I will drop the child to the ground and he or she will delight all of us with peals of laughter—loud and clear. I have lifted my two daughters and my three grandchildren. Veda enjoys this and will appeal to me to lift her. Somewhere there is a snap of PPR lifting the kids on his right palm.

A time-honoured game is 'Jamh Jamh Kuthirey'. The Grandpa sits on a chair, asks the child to place his or her feet one on each of his feet and lifts it to a height of 12 inches and shouts 'Jamh Jamh Kuthirey' and speedily drops the child making it ever so happy. This is one of Veda's favourite hobby—horse.

Veda continues to go for morning walks with her grandma and introduces her to a hundred friends—Rohan Nilay is a huge complex. The friends say, "Hey, Veda" or "Hello, Veda" and stand by for a minute or two. A slightly elder girl Ashna comes home daily to play with Veda for about two hours. Both have extended dialogue—she perfectly understands Vedu—as she calls her.

Among Veda's favourites is 'Ambuchi', which is an abbreviation of Ambuja Chithi—my wife's younger sister. She is a great lover of kids, running a school for small kids. Ambuchi has taught Veda a number of songs, which the child recites vigorously, gloriously, erroneously!

Veda is computer savvy! When Pushpa has put for Veda 'Barney', she enjoys for some time and when she gets bored, she tugs at her Patti—"Come! Come!" She indicates clearly that she must remove the boring CD; she points to a button, which when pressed ejects the cassette. Pushpa has a pouch that carries nearly 20 CDs, and this Veda examines and picks out the 7th item and asks her Patti to put it inside the laptop. Hey! Presto—we hear nursery rhymes 'Baa Baa Black Sheep'. The child dances with joy, and in the adjoining room where I am reading the latest book about Dr Rangarajan, I can hear peals of laughter.

Esther Williams was famous for her film Bathing Beauty, which ran for six months in Bombay's Metro cinema. But the Esther Williams of Rohan Nilay is more charming and vastly more entertaining. She calls it her 'shower'—she sits in a huge tub up to the brim in water and splashes vigorously. By the time the bath is over, every square inch of the huge bathroom is dripping with water. Drying Veda and pushing her into some attire is a modern *bhagiratha prayatna*. Veda runs all over the very spacious house and by the time the great feat of putting her nappy is achieved, there is a strident cry for 'Milk'!

Time flies by deliciously and delightfully for the grandparents in the company of this imp—overflowing with vim and bounce and an abundant sense of the comic. May these grow and may Veda continue entertaining her vibrant parents and the speedily enervating oldies like her grandparents.

36 Miss Kim

She is Miss Kim.

She is a Vietnamese.

She is a tonsorial artist in Sunnyvale, California.

Can I call her a barb-ress—a female barber?

(I must ask my good 'grammar' friend Lawrence in Trivandrum whether there is such a word—emperor - empress and so, barber-barbress.)

I went this morning to 'Silk Cuts'—a barber shop. A spacious affair—40 feet by 40 feet, well lit and well ventilated.

Only two elevated chairs. I found a lady sitting on one and a young lady attending to her hair.

I waited and found the November 2008 issue of *Reader's Digest*. I read one article and hoped another barber will arrive and my chance will arise. But no second barber arrived and I found that the work of that lady customer's coiffure was over.

In a minute this barb-ress said,

"Hi", ever so sweetly and announced, "Now, your turn, Sir."

She must have been 22 years—pleasant smile, in perfect health and in a bob cut style brown hair with strains of gold. Attired in jet black denim jeans and t-shirt, she held a scissor in one hand and towel in the other.

I ascended the elevated chair and was covered with a sparkling new overall, and this lady asked me how I wanted it done.

"Short, military or level?"

I gasped uncomprehendingly and told her calmly,

"I have a dozen hairs. I want you to cut half a dozen and remove the growth round my ears."

She laughed with a tinkle of glass and remarked,

"Hey, you speak good English. Where are you from?"

"India", I declared proudly.

"Oh! Poor country—no water!"

Aghast I asked her, "Who told you?"

"I have seen an Indian film. Lots of ladies walking with pots on heads for miles to get water!"

I asked her, "Any desert in the film you saw?"

"Yes, sir. And so sad I was to see the film."

"Why?" I asked.

"The hero falls in love with the heroine—they dance nicely. And they sing nicely. But the girl's parents don't allow him to marry her. There is a lot of fights, and the hero and heroine are killed. I cried at the end."

Perhaps she saw some film like Rudali or Reshma aur Shera.

I assured her where I come from—Bombay (she has not heard of Thackeray and Mumbai), water is plentiful and lovers can marry without trouble.

She did a good job and with every snip of my denuding hair, she would use a fast whirling mini fan with the result that not one loose piece of hair was attached to me!

No wonder people get their haircuts done on the way to office or during lunch intervals.

However, I went home and in typical Brahmin fashion, dipped all the clothes I wore in water and had my *snanam* (bath) royally.

My engagement with Miss Kim was not terribly hair-raising, but effectively hair-detaching by a barb-ress!

"Don't I look like Paul Newman?", I asked her.

"No, sir. More like Tom Cruise!" she said with a nice smile.

I opened my purse and gave her as instructed by my son-in-law, US dollars 8 plus 2 dollars tips equal to US dollars 10. That was indeed hair-raising!

37 Ishaan the Elf

He is all of three years and stays with his parents in the ground floor flat. Pushpa and Anand are on the first floor. Every evening he will climb the 20 steps and bang the door. The moment we open the door, what begins is a one hour non-stop bout of entertainment, laughter and smiles. A very cheerful, ever smiling lad with doe-like eyes, Ishaan jumps from the word 'go'.

Though he met us for the first time on July 24th, he took to us like a duck to water, especially to Lakshmy for the simple reason that she could converse with him in Marathi. The Dinesh family is from Surat and they are Maharashtrians. Ishaan warmed to me only after a few days since my Marathi was worse than his Swahili. Since Anand's mother is with us, Ishaan had two non-resident grandmas. He would call Lakshmy 'Ajji One' and Radha *mami* 'Ajji Two'.

Pushpa and Anand doted on him, lavished so much affection that he would simply jump into Pushpa's lap and stay there for hours. Anand would hail him as 'Dempoo'. He has a fixed schedule for demanding eatables, which rarely varied. It began with two Parle G biscuits. After demolishing this he would ask for two M&Ms, tiny blue chocolates and finally I would cut some fruit or other. In the beginning he would grab a number of pieces of cut fruits and put in his mouth. I trained him nicely to put piece by piece. Now he will declare, "Ajobaa, one by one!"

After this tiny repast he would play cricket with Anand. Radha *mami* bought for him a squeaking white polka-dotted ball. He would tell Anand *kaka*, play and the two used to better the records of Sachin or Saurav. Incidentally, Ishaan's great grandfather was the famous cricketer of yesteryears, Vijay Hazare. Anand and Ishaan would play to their hearts' content. Meanwhile Alpana, the mother, would appear and take him back home for dinner.

Since I mentioned Anand *kaka*, I must recount an interesting incident. Ishaan called Pushpa -'Pushpa *kaki*' and Anand - 'Anand *kaka*'. When Ishaan became pally with me I told him that in our language '*kaka*' means crow and that he was calling 'Anand a crow'. This was too much for him. He glowered and told me "Kams bad boy." I didn't quite follow the riposte. So I asked Alpana—what is this about Kams? She clarified that Dinesh shows to him stories from the life of Krishna and Kams is identified as a bad boy! So whenever anything disagreeable to him is uttered, he would say "Kams bad boy." The result of my calling Anand a crow was that whenever Ishaan saw me, immediately he would spit out the words "Kams bad boy."

There were other hilarious occasions when Kams would spring in our conversation. If I asked him to deposit the tricycle he had driven in the drawing room, he would obediently put it and declare "Kams nahin karega!" Again Lakshmy was knitting a sweater. He would go to her and say, "Ajji, sweater Ishaanla bantho?" If she did not respond, he would tell "Kamsko sweater math banavo."

I had the unique experience of being fired by Ishaan. One evening Ishaan came as usual, went on with his eating programme and since Anand *kaka* had not returned from office he asked me to play cricket with him. Alas! I was at the middle of a Hercule Poirot story and I did not respond to his request. He went and asked Pushpa to play ball, which she gladly did. Next evening when he came and I was totally free I asked him "Cricket kelu kay?" This was his ready retort. "Tu thikde jaa ani pustak vaacha. Mee Pushpa Kaki ke sath kelu." Fired nicely and squarely by a three year old. Justifiably so!!

Ishaan is not able to pronounce 'R'—he would use the letter 'L'. Since he had broken a windmill, Pushpa had kept the surviving windmill at a height, beyond his reach and told him that the windmill was hot or *garam*. He would come and announce. "Windmill galam hai." Likewise, when Anand and Pushpa had gone for 10 days to Peru, he used to come and play with us and say, "Pushpa Kaki Pelu geli?" Even today, whenever Pushpa is not at home Ishaan will announce "Pushpa Kaki Pelu geli." Every evening Lakshmy would light a lamp and she had warned him not to go near, since it was fire. He called the lamp 'candle' and would ask her to light a 'candle' if she had not already done. He would then declare, "Candle Galam hai."

Ishaan goes to a nearby day-care centre since both the parents work. We will daily get stories of Manju Moushi—what all he had learnt that day, what games he played. During our stay, Ishaan's third birthday celebrations were held and all of us partook of that joy.

We are surely going to Miss Ishaan as he is going to miss us. Ishaan the elf—our bountiful blessings on this pure delight.

ESSAYS »

38 I Love Edison

Thomas Alva Edison (1847-1931) is remembered by all Americans on a single day—his birthday 11th February. This day is declared as National Science Day as a tribute to Edison who had 1093 US patents to his credit. He is publicly remembered for his invention of the bulb and on his birthday, in entire America, all the bulbs are switched on for one full minute as a tribute to Edison. If Americans remember him one day in a year, I always remember him night and day—not for the electric lamp but for the permanent limp in my left leg, which was gifted by him to me. For when and how please read on.

A couple of years ago, as the weary sun wore off after a dreadfully hot day and as dusk descended, my wife switched on the light in the hall. There was a sudden plop sound, a sharp flash and it was as if the good Lord said, "Let there be darkness and there was darkness." Utter stygian darkness as the bulb had fused!

My wife started shouting out the first letter of the alphabet, "A...A...A...A...A." I was in the bedroom and only on its eighth utterance did I hear her and thus, learnt of the sad and untimely demise of the hall bulb. As in the famous Harry Belafonte ditty, "Dear Henry", she shouted, "Fix it. Well fix it. At dusk it should not be dark!" "How else can it be at dusk?" I boldly asked myself.

She promptly produced a bulb and I had no go but to shed light! I dragged a tall stool with three steps and ascended it, taking one step at a time. Alas! The second step was somewhat loose. So I put very little of my weight on it and successfully attained the top. In pitch dark, I put up my right hand and held the bulb. The heat had not worn off. I turned it on its socket clockwise. But it was not easy as I thought it ought to be. Perhaps, I should have turned it anticlockwise! However, I turned it tighter and I heard a slight sound. One of the two connectors had got dislodged and fell on the floor. Now it was easy to turn the bulb and I easily did it and held the dead thing in my hand. This done, the next step was to descend, carefully keeping in mind the loose second step. I did this without much ado and gently placed the fused bulb on the table. I proceeded now, with the new bulb in my right hand and ascended to the top without straining the second step.

Firmly standing on the stool top, I put in the fresh bulb into the socket and gently turned it. I was lucky as the bulb neatly turned semicircle and lodged itself securely. I whistled a happy tune and alighted with force on the second step. It came down with crash and down I fell like a sack of potatoes. All the weight was on my left leg—68 kg for those keen students of anatomy! I felt a stinging pain.

Meanwhile, I asked my wife to put on the switch. As she did, the hall was bathed in a flood of light. I had succeeded in fitting a new bulb. But my victory turned to ashes as I found I could not get up. I was lifted up by my wife and daughter. I was deposited in a chair. The pain mounted like the temperature mounting in a desert as noon approaches.

A doc was summoned and that worthy, after some knocks and twists and turns pronounced that I had a broken femur. I was in a plaster cast for six weeks and now I walk with a limp.

But I will never forget Thomas Alva Edison and his 'Incantation to Incandescence'.

39 On Loving *Bhel*

When the portions relating to gastronomical developments in the history of India come to be written, Mumbai will feature as the home and haven of lovers of *bhel puri*. Never has an article of consumption provided pleasure in such an abundant measure, in such a short time, to so many people. Mumbai's *bhel puri* betters the record of either Kolkata's *rossogolla* (notwithstanding its dollar-earning aptitude) or Chennai's *idli sambhar* (despite its ubiquity).

The origin of *bhel puri* is lost in the mists of antiquity. However, history plays a passive role in determining our regimen. Thus, while people never bother to enquire into who the first *bhel*-eater was, they are happy that *bhel* exists for their delight.

Now, *bhel puri* is a delectable mixture of *sev, poha*, onion, boiled potatoes, amply aided by *khara* or *meetha chutney*, which lends to it a specially agreeable taste. The mixing of *bhel* is a peculiar art, to the acquisition of which much effort and skill must be devoted. Indeed, it is given to the few alone to attain perfection in this field. The constituents must be combined in proper proportions. A little too much of the one or a little too less of the other, may rob the mixture of its magical property.

The vision of *bhel*-lovers consuming *bhel* is an unfailing source of endless delight. The sight of a *bhel puriwala* stirs the mortal frame and feeds the sacred flame of the *bhel*-eating gentry. The lover doubles up his pace and, in a second, is by the side of the *bhel puriwala*.

The *bhel wala*, usually an unkempt, unshaven fellow, is all smiles baring his few pan-stained teeth. He prepares the mixture and hands it over on a piece of paper or a leaf. The function of a spoon is served by a *puri*—a flat, hard, tasty substance, eminently fitted to perform this function.

Bhel-lovers, like all lovers, shed all codes of civilised conduct and gobble up uncouthly immense quantities of the substance with remarkable ease. Indeed, the tongue serves as cleaner of the hands. Once he or she is full to the brim with this delicacy, the *bhel*-lover appears as if charged with a sense of divinity and bestows his bounteous sight on this barren world.

The significance of *bhel* lies in the fact that it is at once economical and bears about it a high satisfaction yielding quotient. We will leave it to the interested student to strike at a scientific formula relating *bhel* consumption to the accompanying satisfaction.

Now, *bhel* is consumed by different persons for different reasons. Fat men assert that it contains onion, and hence improves the prospects of their slimming. Lean souls, on the other hand, with equal vehemence maintain the opposed view, drawing pointed attention to the carbohydrates content of the combination, and swallow it with glee.

A recent survey of the eating habits of a cross-section of the cosmopolitan content of Mumbai revealed startling results. The report is an impartial document and is highly rewarding, and is a must for the interested student and the layman. The report points out *inter alia* that a majority of *bhel*-lovers belong to the fair sex.

Without fear of contradiction, we can state that next to make-up, women love *bhel*. I know of one lady who adds as much to her weight by consuming large quantities of *bhel*.

When her husband—a Government servant—was transferred from Mumbai, she sustained a severe shock and only after repeated remonstrance from her otherwise devoted hubby, did she condescend to accompany him to *bhel*-less Bhilai.

It is my earnest desire to see her, bereft of the very staff and prop of her life—the all consuming *bhel*. I suppose she, like Kalidasa's Yaksha in Ramagiri, roams over Bhilai weak and emaciated.

40 The Colonel and I

To arrive hopefully is better than to travel. I had settled down in my seat and sent up a prayer of thanks to the Almighty for the excellence of the facilities provided by the Indian Railways.

Little did I reckon with the fact that peace and tranquility, comfort and ease were ephemeral, evanescent wisps of the mind.

We had barely traversed a 100 miles when a new star swam into our horizon—a Colonel, in fact, a retired one. He was a hefty man with bushy eye brows and sharp angular eyes, which could plumb your depths. He had a resounding voice and I dreamt he would fit ideally for shouting slogans at the numerous demonstrations arranged by the trade unions in Mumbai.

But it was more than voice or noise. Though the hour was late, he wanted to unburden himself of fragments of autobiography. A born patient listener, I had not the heart nor courage to say 'No'.

Hailing from a martial stock, he had undergone training at Sandhurst as well as West Point. He had travelled from China to Peru. He claimed to have been a leading participant in the victorious battle of Gallipoli. I was certain this event dated back to 1915-16 and, in fact, the British were routed by the Turks and had to be evacuated.

When I interjected to display this piece of knowledge, he pounced on me with feline ferocity and gave a lecture on my profound ignorance.

He was livid with impotent rage. My protests became murmurs and eventually, I was reduced to silence. Pleading fatigue, I fell into slumber.

My colonel was an early bird. When I woke up I found he had washed, shaved, changed clothes and applied a pungent scent with which I promptly declared to be in disagreement. This time he was not angry. He beamed with joy and descanted on the virtues of tolerance, the need to accept variety and abjure stubbornness.

He offered me a cup of hot tea from a flask and plied me with some sweets and biscuits. I drew his attention to his outburst of the previous night. He apologised handsomely and we became rather chummy. During the entire day, he was in excellent temper and did his best to spread joy and happiness.

The thought that I had to spend another night in his company found me in the grip of a vague, unnamed fear. Here was a cross between a tiger and the lamb, a curious mixture of the fierce and the docile—a modern version of Dr Jekyll and Mr Hyde.

On the second night he was in worse temper than on the previous night. Now his subject was religion. He claimed to be an adherent of Zen Buddhism and derided all other religions. When I meekly pointed out that a military career was incompatible with Buddhist tenets and that Zen Buddhism was an inbred religion lacking the catholicity of Hinduism, he adverted to the evils of our religion and asserted that salvation lay in the path of Buddha. He left me no choice. For a few hours I was an ardent Zen Buddhist.

It was with a sigh of relief that I saw Madras Central. It was morn by then. My friend had taken on his jovial aspect. He invited me to visit him at an address at Tambaram. I promptly forgot the address and hopped into a cab, resting and content with the thought that I had arrived hopefully though not travelled so.

41 Operation Send-Off

The eastern sky is resplendent with roseate streaks of a fresh day. The birds chirp merrily. There is a nip in the air. The scene is in the city of the reclining lord—Trivandrum.

A child is comfortably sleeping—encased in a thick cotton bed-sheet aided by a woollen blanket. You can see neither the head nor the legs of the child for she believes in full protection.

"Get up, Pushpa", booms her mother's voice. "Pushpa, Pushpa, it's six already." No effect on the subject!

"How many times have I told you not to cover the head and breathe foul air?" Any number of times, but has the small one heard even once. I wonder!

"I am defeated", she says and then turns to me. "A...A...A (why do fathers get called by the 1st alphabet!!). You wake her up!"

No sooner said than done! I just lift her and plant her on her feet! This does not mean she is awake. Only she is not lying down.

At this point, it would be in order to describe 'P'. She is in a polka-dot pajama suit, the buttons not put, as it was when she went to bed. She has discarded her ribbons and her hair is overflowing her tiny head and it will be an achievement to see through her bushy growth—even if she has opened her eyes!

"You have gone early to bed. So you must get up early." declares the mother. Where is this law enunciated? In Manu Smriti, the Talmud, Hammurabi's Code? I don't know.

Cleaning teeth takes some time. The next major operation is bathing. Search for the requisite apparel calls for Himalayan endeavour! Though the mother has neatly arranged all the items the previous evening, the little one cannot locate her towel—as she has made a glorious mess of the arrangement.

Bath is over in five minutes. Out emerges our little one with not one drop of water having fallen on her face! Quite an achievement, this!

'Operation Uniform'. If the shoes are available, the socks are not traceable. Inevitably, only one of a pair is available. The neatly pressed white *dupatta* is properly poised on the uniform but to place it securely, a pair of safety pins is essential. But where are the pins?

God only knows. It is the proverbial hunt for the needle in the haystack. At last the resourceful mother produces it out of her necklace and the problem is solved.

Suddenly Pushpa announces it is mass PT today. "I have to wear canvas shoes, white uniform!" A quick transformation takes place—in a trice with verbal firing from the annoyed parents.

As with all children, it's an achievement to inject food.

By now it is 8.30—time to take off to school. Pushpa has set off for school. "Amma", she shouts, "I have forgotten the handkerchief." A quick search and she sails off.

Another successful send-off!

42 My Sporting Career

You have, of course, not heard of the MAC. I shall enlighten you. It was the Matunga Athletic Club, guaranteed to transform spindly, spare lads into mighty, muscular men. Located opposite the Ruia College, along the rail track, it had an array of remarkable equipment, dumbbells, stretchable rubber belts, skipping ropes, etc. As a young lad I used to stand outside the club rapt in total admiration of the young men, duly well oiled, bursting with muscle all over, performing gymnastics of every kind and calisthenics of every hue. I longed to be a member. One of the legendary members was Shri K. Hariharan, who later on distinguished himself as Principal of the Reserve Bank Staff College. Of him, presently.

Being a family friend, I pestered Hariharan to enrol me. He opined that I was too young and any way, that evening the Club was to felicitate that year's 'Mr India' and would I care to come? The day was dreadfully long for me and I paid no attention to what my English teacher- Shri Doraiswamy Iyer—who looked like Julius Caesar had to say of.

"...The Daniel comes to judgment." When he asked, who said this, where and when, I promptly blurted out 'MAC' and got equally promptly rapped. Now it was 5 pm, I was to be found squatting in front of the first row. Quite a crowd of Samsons, Herculeses and Ulyssesses it was! Hariharan, welcomed the national award winner, gave him a present and asked him to reveal the secret of his health. I was all keyed up and listened with tremendous enthusiasm.

The muscle man advocated, apart from a disciplined system of exercise, a dietary prescription, which simply bowled me over! "Every night", he said, "fill a glass of plain water, drop a small piece of *gur*, and allow it to settle down. The next morning, after cleaning your teeth, the first thing you must imbibe is this concoction—and not tea. Not coffee." Such sound advice needed to be immediately followed to make me a powerful person. Alas! man proposes and God disposes! I must at this stage declare my great love for *gur*, even as a boy. As I inaugurated this new 'Get Strong' scheme, I would religiously fill a glass with limpid clear water and assiduously chip a piece of *gur* and lovingly deposit in the glass. But behold, what happened, during this process. Wily Oscar Wilde had said, "The best way to get rid of a temptation is to yield to it." Fascinated by the golden substance, I used to help myself with large quantities of it at night, while restricting it to a small piece along with water overnight. Scarcely 15 days later, I had to be marched to the doctor, who ordered a strict diet, totally abjuring sweets, including *gur*. Alas!

A few years later, Hariharan helped me secure admission. Beginning with simple physical exercises, I progressed to performing on the parallel bars, which were full five feet from the ground. On one occasion, as I was swinging, a mischievous boy lifted me up by my legs; my hands got dislodged, and I fell from the Olympian height on my chin. Instantly I saw Saturn and Jupiter hurtling past me, a terribly bright solar flare—almost a remarkable replica of Carl Sagan's 'Cosmos'. I woke up—after three hours of unconsciousness—and was discharged from the hospital with four stitches on my chin—the marks of which I still carry—a sort of Arjuna Award!

My career in the school hockey team was gloriously short-lived. As I ran after the ball, weaving my stick with skill and dexterity, the leading light of the opposite team shot like a meteor into my ken and his massive stick hit my solar plexus initially and my leg slightly later with considerable finesse, and I collapsed like a bag of golf balls. I had to be lifted and deposited and medically assisted massively, as I had sustained a fracture of the leg. I convalesced in bed with a plaster cast for over a month. So much for a budding Dhyan Chand!

Correspondence

43 C. Rajagopalachari

P.P. Ramachandran
Bombay

October 8, 1969

Shri C. Rajagopalachari,
Madras

Dear Sir,

A pertinent request.

I have been closely watching your brilliant campaign against the present Indian Government. You have turned the searchlight of criticism on the Government's various failings and obviously believe it to be wicked. Amidst the controversies you indulge in with the spokesmen of the Nehru Government (including Nehru), I am somewhat surprised that you continue to enjoy an award accorded to you by this Government.

I would suggest to you to return the Bharat Ratna Award. You have the glorious and shining example of Mahatma Gandhi—by whom you swear—who, when disgusted with the British Government returned on August 1, 1920 the Kaiser-i-Hind Gold Medal and other decorations he had won in Africa.

Please do not take me amiss.

Yours faithfully,

Raman

C. Rajagopalachari
Personal

9.10.69

Dear Shri,

Your letter of October 8. My having the decoration or giving it up will make not the slightest difference either to me or the Government. The parallel you cite does not apply. The action you suggest would be silly exhibitionism and a symptom of foolishness. The prevailing atmosphere of exhibitionism makes you suggest this.

Yours sincerely,

C. Rajagopalachari

44 Jeffrey Archer

P.P. Ramachandran,
Bombay
25-6-1986

Dear Archer,

It may perhaps bring you some joy to learn that readers of your books are legion in India. Ever since I bought your 'Kane and Abel', I have become a dedicated target of Jeffrey's archery. I must confess a preference to your 'Not a Penny More, Not a Penny Less', which revealed your rich sense of humour and almost a near-Wodehousian wit.

Only last week we could lay our hands on 'A Matter of Honour', which has been compared in the blurb to 'Thirty Nine Steps', but in my view is in the best traditions of Eric Ambler. I must say that I have enjoyed reading this novel, which has nuggets of information (like the floors of the Pentagon). Now I have detected certain confusion in the vehicles used by Romanov in his pursuit of Adam. The page numbers referred by me are in the paperback Coronet edition (An average Indian cannot dream of buying a hard-bound!).

On p.197, Romanov says, "I want a fast car, and more important, a superb driver?"

A page later, p. 198, Romanov says, "Faster!" aware that it was not possible as the Ambassador's driver was proving to be a consummate professional.

On p. 205, Romanov asks the driver to get the car and you write “A few minutes later the Mercedes drew up by Romanov’s side.”

“... the heavy Mercedes took another kilometer before the car slowed to a complete stop” (p.211).

Well, Mr. Archer, Romanov can become Rosenbaum in a jiffy, but I doubt whether an Ambassador can become a Mercedes!

I shall be grateful for a line in reply.

Yours sincerely,

P.P. Ramachandran

Jeffrey Archer,
18th July 1986

P.P. Ramachandran Esq.,

Dear Mr Ramachandran,

Thank you for your recent letter and the kind words concerning ‘A Matter of Honour’.

I am very glad to hear that it has reached India safely and you have enjoyed reading it. I have taken on board the points you made about the Mercedes and will certainly bear them in mind for a future edition.

Yours sincerely,

Jeffrey Archer

45 H.R.F. Keating

P.P. Ramachandran
18-12-1972

My dear Keating,

I have just finished reading your 'Inspector Ghote Goes by Train' and would like to draw your attention to certain violations of 'unity of place'.

On page 12, begins the momentous journey of the Calcutta Mail. "The long train crept hardly more than trotting pace out of Bombay. Slowly it gathered speed as it moved on to the centre tracks past the frequent suburban stations, Masjid, Sandhurst Road High Level, Dockyard Road, Reay Road, Cotton Green."

Firstly, Central Railway is split up into: (a) Main Line and (b) Harbour Branch. On the former run all long distance trains including Ghote's Calcutta Mail. The stations common to both the lines are only Bombay VT and Masjid. All the other stations mentioned on page 12 are on the Harbour Branch by which the Calcutta Mail does not run. For your information, I have drawn the sketch of the two lines, which mingle at Kurla. When you bring out a new edition or paperback please change the stations to read as "Masjid, Sandhurst Road Low Level, Byculla, Chinchpokli, Currey Road, Parel, Dadar".

A passenger by Calcutta Mail cannot see P and O Dock Yard at Mazagon nor the Sewri Cemetery. Please amend pages 12 and 13 suitably.

Again, who told you that the sacred thread of a Brahmin is black (p. 12)? It is always white and Brahmins scrupulously keep it white.

May I have a word in reply?

Yours sincerely,

P.P. Ramachandran

3/Jan/73

Dear Ramachandran,

May I, you ask in your letter in December 18, have a word in reply. Indeed, you may. And that word is: thank you.

Writing of Bombay in distant London, there are many occasions when I am not sure of an exact fact. Usually, I either find someone I can ask or I contrive to omit the detail. But occasionally, I have to take a risk.

A long scrutiny of the map convinced me (wrongly, alas) that of the two lines out of VT station, the Calcutta Express was more likely to take the one I chose. However, I am delighted to hear which is in fact the correct choice, and I believe your letter came in time for me to make the correction in the paperback, which Penguin is to issue in due course. Sadly, the American in hardback is already in print.

I cannot think how it was that I got onto my head that Brahmin's sacred thread is black. But I saw it clearly as such. It is strange the tricks the mind can play. And again be sure, the change will be made wherever it can be corrected.

Perhaps, one day I shall succeed in coming to Bombay and will be able to bring into clear focus all the many sights I have at the moment in my mind's eye. If I do come, I shall take the liberty of writing to you so that we may perhaps meet. In the meantime, Collins have recently published 'Inspector Ghote Trusts the Heart' and I hope that you will find pleasure in it- but no errors.

Yours sincerely,

H.R.F. Keating

CORRESPONDENCE »

46 C. Rajagopalachari

Reserve Bank of India
March 24, 1968.

Shri C. Rajagopalachari,

Dear Sir,

We are a small group of employees of the Reserve Bank of India on training here for a short period. We are eager to meet you, talk with you and secure your blessings. We shall be thankful if you can fix up an appointment for us on any date from April 2 to April 11, 1968, convenient to you.

Yours sincerely

P.P. Ramachandran

26th March 68

Dear Sir,

Your kind letter. My blessings must be taken by you in absentia. I am not able to spare energy for personal meeting. If blessings have any power, they will operate across space. My best wishes to you all.

Yours sincerely,

C. Rajagopalachari

47 Khushwant Singh

P.P. Ramachandran
15-6-1993

My dear Khushwant Singh,

Why do you allow others to pull your leg?

In your latest 'With Malice towards One and All', there is a story about Winston Churchill, of a certain lady who would not come into contact with his politics or moustache.

It is universally known that Churchill never had a moustache. One could attach as much credibility to Winston's moustache as to a clean shaven Kushwant Singh.

For God's sake, check your contributor's profile, before you print.

Yours sincerely,

P.P. Ramachandran

Shri Khushwant Singh

My dear P.P.,

I knew Churchill did not have a moustache (he came for a reception in India House). I let the story go to find out how many readers would spot the error. One did.

Yours truly,

Khushwant Singh

48 S. Radhakrishnan

Dr. S. Radhakrishnan
August 25, 1967

Dear Sir,

I have just read your book 'Religion in Changing World'. It is like a breath of fresh air in an atmosphere stifled by doubt and despondency. It beckons one hopefully as does a light at the end of a long and dark tunnel.

The first step to progress is clearly understanding and it is this which has prompted me to take this liberty of penning these lines. There is a passage in the book, which has left me confused. I would seek your assistance in clarifying the point.

Warning the elders not to be daunted by failures in their effort to protect the youth (to whom I belong) against the folly and stupidity of their elders, you write "It is better sometimes to fail than to succeed in doing harm" (p. 152).

One thought it is always better to fail in doing harm. There are no exceptional concessions here.

With Best Regards

Yours sincerely,

P.P. Ramachandran

August 28, 1967.

Dear Sri Ramachandran,

Quite true; it is good that we always fail to do harm, but sometimes we succeed in doing harm. So we should try to reduce that number also and see that we don't succeed in doing harm.

Yours sincerely

S. Radhakrishnan

CORRESPONDENCE »

49 Paul W. Gallico

P.P. Ramachandran,
January 9, 1967

My dear Mr Gallico,

I am one of your fervent admirers and sincerely believe that humanity owes you a debt, which will never be repaid. Your books—which have won immediate and increasing approbation from Indian readers represent a fund of entertainment and wisdom into which we can delve to our hearts' content. One cannot but fall in love with Mrs Harris, become fascinated with the adventures of Jennie, get caught in admiration of Alexander Hero, follow with genuine zest the solution to the problem of the survival of the Barbary apes and finally become infatuated with Mopsy (who is one-up over Adam).

Now I have a problem in connection with your book 'Trial by Terror', the Penguin edition of which I bought recently (Indians are still in the Penguin stage!). Andreas Ordy, Minister of Affairs in the Cabinet of the Communist Government of Hungary, is hunting for his one-time secretary Gabor Lajos, who has in his possession incriminating evidence about the Minister's Titoist activities. Lajos is in Paris, masquerading as Grisha; his wife bakes cakes and his daughter Ilya Lagos works as a model named Alaine in the dress house of Rene Vesoul. And according to Thyra, Alaine's pictures are blazoned in the pages of Paris *Vogue*, "There she is", she said, at a full page of the model pictured wearing one of the Vesoul afternoon creations of the past winter. "That's Alaine. And this one, and this one too. He uses her for all his sophisticated creations..." (p.175—Chapter 21).

Surely it is not naive to believe that Ordy and his extraordinary men can identify not only Lajos, but his wife and daughter Ilya Lajos. With Ilya's identity being flaunted so publicly, it would be child's play for the Hungarians to kidnap this lady and thereby capture Lajos and execute him. Why was this not done? Or is it wrong to believe that Hungarian secret police on the look out for a wanted man thumb the pages of Paris *Vogue* and find their wanted man's daughter in sophisticated clothes?

Yours sincerely,
P.P. Ramachandran

3rd February, 1967

Dear Ramachandran,

I do thank you for your letter, which shows a most gratifying acquaintance with my characters.

Yours is a pretty clever analysis of a weakness in the 'Trial by Terror' story, which never struck me or anybody else, for that matter, and I should say you are the first one to have discovered it, and well done you! And for heaven's sake don't tell anybody else!

On the other hand, in extenuation I can only suggest that once Lajos and his family vanished from Vienna, they dropped out of sight; the arm of the Hungarian police did not extend as far as Paris, or the pages of Elle and Vogue. I also put it to you that at the time of the Tito affair, Ilya Lajos was a little girl and there is no reason why even a Hungarian Secret agent, thumbing through a fashion magazine and looking at the picture of a famous model should identify her with the child who was, let us say, five or six years old at the time of an incident.

Anyway, it's fun to have someone read one of my books so closely and I thank you for the trouble you took.

With all good wishes,

Yours sincerely,

Paul W. Gallico

P.P. Ramachandran
2nd March, 1972

Dear Mr Gallico,

Your 'Zoo Gang' have just landed in Bombay and as a typical Gallico slave, I devoured the book in one sitting! In the process I acquired the powers of a hawk, and I have detected a certain mixing up of the vehicles owned by the different characters. And here it goes!

1. Captain Claude Scobide

a) "...Roquebrun concluded, and watched seriously through the window as the captain marched to his black Citroen and departed"-p.10

b) "The two men shook hands and through the window the Colonel watched the inconspicuous detective depart in his inconspicuous Peugeot" - p.39

2. Colonel Pierre Roquebrun

a) "Colonel Roquebrun drove his Simca station wagon up the twisting road into the hills behind Cannes..."-p. 17

b) 'He (i.e. the Colonel) packed a bag, and leaving both his cars in the garage–his black Mercedes as well as the Peugeot station wagon—he took a taxi to Nice..." –p.77

You say both his cars, but we have three vehicles viz., (1) Simca station wagon, (2) Peugeot station wagon and (3) black Mercedes.

3. Sarah Howard

a) "A car crunched to a halt...Colonel Roquebrun...saw the gleaming cream and chrome Jaguar of Sarah Howard."-p.2

Those who sent the ransom note to Sarah Howard ought to know the colour of her car. Yet the ransom note reads, *inter alia* "when your father arrives in the morning bring him in your white car to the cross-roads sign below Piol..." p.22

I am prepared to believe that Scobide, Roquebrun as well as Howard have more than one vehicle, but it does appear to me that a little careful editing (especially about both the cars of Roquebrun) would have removed this confusion.

In this connection, I recall your letter to me dated March 14, 1970 where, in you state, "All the points in your interesting letter are well taken care and show how sloppy a writer can get and why they have to have editors. The only thing that does not show is why the editors do not edit".

Likewise I had pointed out and you had handsomely acknowledged the weakness in your 'Trial by Terror' story (refer to your letter dated February 3, 1967).

May I take the liberty of offering my services in ensuring that such flaws do not occur in your forthcoming books? My only reward would be that I read the book before it is launched into a rapacious world.

With regards,

Yours sincerely,

P.P. Ramachandran

France
March 10, 1972

Dear Mr Ramachandran,

By golly, you are marvellous. You win again. I wish you were sitting in the office of my publishers, Heinemann Ltd., in London, instead of your bank in Bombay.

I can only bow my head in shame, and to assist the editors at Heinemann's to bow theirs, I shall send them a photocopy of your letter on the strange assortment of vehicles that turned up in 'Zoo Gang'.

As you can see from the typing, I am without a secretary for the moment and that is no help either, but beginning next week I shall have a new one, a girl with a good eye for errors and so perhaps, my next book will get a clean bill of health from you.

But this is just to say that I do appreciate your writing.

Of course, I could maintain that Captain Scobide always changed cars so as to maintain his disguise as a tourist, but I'm afraid that wouldn't wash. I am the fellow who drives the inconspicuous Peugeot station wagon. But Colonel ought to make up his mind.

You must be quite a guy.

Thanks again.

Yours sincerely,

Paul W. Gallico

50 Harry Keating

P.P. Ramachandran
Mumbai, 400054
November 17, 1976.

Dear Keating,

You wrote to me (on 3-1-1975) .... "Collins have recently published 'Inspector Ghote Trusts the Heart' and I hope you find pleasure in it – but no errors".

Denied the Collin's edition by consideration of the purse, I could obtain the Penguin paperback only two days ago and hasten to assure you, I was captivated by the elfin charm of the Inspector and his new adventure.

Alas, a few errors have crept in. You have got all your arithmetic muddled up! Here it goes.

Page 38

'The criminal would tell Desai where to leave the sum of twenty lakhs of rupees, probably in used 100–rupee notes–two thousand of them...." Two thousand hundred is only 2 lakh. Say 'Twenty thousand rupee notes or two thousand thousand rupee notes'.

Page 96

"A hundred rupees, just one of many notes that the proprietor of Trst-X had counted out to make up that sum one hundred times greater that he had been willing to pay to save little Pidku."

Hundred times hundred is 10,000 and not one lakh—the amount Desai was willing to pay for Pidku. Write 'A hundred rupees...to make up that sum thousand times greater'.

As the book was published in 1972, one presumes that the events relate to that year or earlier. There are several occasions when the ransom amount is composed of fifty rupee notes (pp.39, 58, 59, 126). Actually, the fifty rupee note was issued for the first time in India on May 17, 1975. Thus, though foresight is shown, facts are not described. It would be better to change it to ten-rupee notes.

May I take this opportunity of requesting you to send me a copy of the obituary note you wrote on that 'Mistress of Mystery Agatha Christie'? Try as hard as I did, I could not locate it.

Yours sincerely,

P.P. Ramachandran

London
2. Dec/76

Dear Ramachandran,

Thank you indeed for your letter so charmingly and tactfully pointing out my arithmetical errors. In your profession, you will hardly be able to believe it, but I am so bad at figures that I am all too apt to forget what a lakh is that the source of all the trouble, I suspect, except for the forecast 50 rupee notes (and I cannot think how that occurred as I am generally punctilious in looking up a fact like that).

Let me tell you that when I visited Bombay for the first time in October 1974, I lunched with the sons of a film producer (who shall be nameless) to discuss the possible purchase of rights in some of my books. I was pressed to name a figure and, owing to my having as I subsequently realised a weakness at Math, I divided the sum I

had in mind by 10 because I was translating pounds into rupees and thousands into lakhs. I asked for such a tiny amount that in an instant a hand shot out across the table and an enthusiastic voice said, "Mr Keating, we have a deal!" Mercifully, perhaps the books have not really proved suitable for a Hindi film, as you can imagine.

Anyway, I have carefully noted the alteration you suggest and when an opportunity arises, I shall take care to incorporate them.

Now, about the obituary of Agatha Christie I think I must have mentioned. Alas I wrote nothing. I did, when she died appear on television here to sum up her career and also gave a brief radio talk, but not a word in indissoluble print. I am just completing the editing of a book to be called 'Agatha Christie; first lady of crime', which Weidenfeld and Nicholson are to publish next spring. But I rather fear that 'consideration of the purse' will make it an unwarranted expenditure for all, but the most wealthy in India. Perhaps some library or club will give you a chance of seeing it.

With many thanks for your interest, and for your expression of pleasure about 'trusts the heart' (In April, I believe, Penguin Bats Fly Up For Inspector Ghote).

Yours sincerely,

Harry Keating

51 Pope John Paul II

Bombay
12-12-1994

Revered Holiness,

Ever since I saw your beatific smile at distant Trivandrum, I have been following your trail in search of 'Pacem in Terris'. I was deeply moved to read portions of your 'Crossing the Threshold of Hope'.

Don't you think it is a tragedy that while the son of the God rode free on a donkey, the Pontiff has to ride in a bullet proof Popomobile? I pray for the day when you can walk free.

I wish you a Merry Christmas, a Happy New Year and seek your blessings.

Yours sincerely,

P.P. Ramachandran

Secretariat of State
First section—General Affairs
From the Vatican,
Christmas 1994

His Holiness Pope John Paul II expresses his gratitude for the kind greetings sent to him for Christmas and the New Year. He greatly appreciates the sentiments, which prompted this thoughtful gesture.

Upon all who have remembered him during this holy season, His Holiness invokes an abundance of joy and peace in Jesus Christ—the Icarnate Word.

Monsignor L. Sandri

Assessor

Index